Should W
Household Debts?

The Future of Capitalism series

Johnna Montgomerie

Should We Abolish
Household Debts?

polity

First published in 2019 by Polity Press

Polity Press
65 Bridge Street
Cambridge CB2 1UR, UK

Polity Press
101 Station Landing
Suite 300
Medford, MA 02155, USA

ISBN-13: 978-1-5095-2539-3
ISBN-13: 978-1-5095-2540-9 (pb)

A catalogue record for this book is available from the British Library.

Library of Congress Cataloging-in-Publication Data
Names: Montgomerie, Johnna, author.
Title: Should we abolish household debts? / Johnna Montgomerie.
Description: Medford, MA : Polity, 2018. | Series: The future of capitalism |
    Includes bibliographical references and index.
Identifiers: LCCN 2018045028 (print) | LCCN 2018046565 (ebook) | ISBN
    9781509525430 (Epub) | ISBN 9781509525393 (hardback) | ISBN 9781509525409
    (paperback)
Subjects: LCSH: Debt--Social aspects. | Mortgage loans. | Consumer credit. |
    Debt cancellation. | BISAC: POLITICAL SCIENCE / Public Policy / Economic
    Policy.
Classification: LCC HG3701 (ebook) | LCC HG3701 .M626 2018 (print) | DDC
    332.7/43--dc23
LC record available at https://lccn.loc.gov/2018045028

Typeset in 11 on 15 Sabon by
Servis Filmsetting Ltd, Stockport, Cheshire
Printed and bound in Great Britain by T.J. International Limited

For further information on Polity, visit our website:
politybooks.com

This book is dedicated to my Dad, John Montgomerie. Thank you for cancelling my student debt, you always inspire me to think big.

Contents

Tables and Figures

Tables

Figures

Acknowledgements

My biggest intellectual debts are to Ann Pettifor, Steve Keen and Will Davies, who, each in their own way, informed my thinking for this book. I have benefited greatly from intellectual interactions with Daniela Tepe-Belfrage, Clea Bourne (and our Heretical Finance Reading Group), Chris Harker, and Ben Fine – to name just those who gave me feedback. This book also owes a debt to the many civil society organizations I have learned so much from over the past few years: New Economics Foundation, Centre for Responsible Credit, Jubilee Debt Campaign, Positive Money, Trade Union Congress, Finance Innovation Lab, FairForYou, Debt Resistance UK. However, I save my most sincere thanks and appreciation for those who helped me find the time to write this book while pregnant and after having my third baby: my husband, Sam, who supported me with countless hours of childcare and many takeaway dinners, and my neighbours Megan and Rachel, who mucked in many times when I was in a pinch.

Introduction

This book seeks to answer a simple question: Should we abolish household debts? The short answer is 'yes'. Why? Because we are currently living through the protracted afterlife of the 2008 financial crisis, in a zombie-like economy that lacks vitality, growth, renewal, investment, diversification. The debts of households (or the segment of private debt held by individuals who organize as households) exist as an echo from a time already lived, and of a growth already measured, of a credit-fuelled bubble that already burst. Debt is producing wealth for some and harm for many others. We must break through the fog of the zombie economy by accepting the economic, political, cultural and psychological consequences of widespread indebtedness within the economy and within society at large. The cumulative effects of debt manifest as generalized 'financial melancholia' when our collective political economic future is predicated on always having to pay for the past (Davies, Montgomerie, and Wallin 2015). Abolishing household debts is the most direct way of ending the financial crisis that has held households for more than a decade in its grip, since this crisis is caused by their having to continue to pay their debts while absorbing both the shock of economic downturn and the costs of austerity. Meanwhile the lenders and the entire financial sector received bailouts first, then direct financing from the central banks. We are told that these measures are necessary to protect the finance sector from the dire effects of the financial crisis they caused. I contend that abolishing household debt would be more effective than the current monetary policy at ending the wider economic stagnation caused by the 2008 financial crisis (Weale 2016). More importantly, abolishing household debt would trigger the end of our long-term dependence on debt more readily than the current financial reform agenda would.

This book makes the case for household debt cancellation on the basis of my 15 years of experience in researching and writing on the phenomenon of the rising household debt in Anglo-American economies. Put simply, led by the United States and the United Kingdom, the English-speaking countries with colonial ties to Britain demonstrate similar economic trajectories of using debt instead of wages to drive growth over the past 25 years. I have worked with academics in the fields of finance, policymaking, think tanks and civil society organizations, in order to improve my understanding of the many facets of debt and its effects on economy and society. Debt is not a universal 'thing', its effects are not uniform, and it matters what other factors are at play in the economy and in society. I bring together this cumulative knowledge, aiming to provide an easily accessible account of why cancelling household debt is the most direct route to a better future, one free of the current, deep-seeded dependence on debt and of the financial melancholia it creates.

The process of understanding the effects of debt and of locating the harm it can generate begins with the everyday life experiences of those people who have personal experience of debt dependence: they cannot buy a home without taking on more debt than they can afford; they can get a university degree only by taking on more debt than they will earn upon graduation; they borrow to get through a family member's illness or period of unemployment; credit cards get them to the end of each month; or they live on their overdraft. For many, debt is a necessity, not an option. Others are not adversely affected by debt; these tend to be older, to live near a major city, or to have wealthy parents. For the baby boomer generation, and even for most of Generation X, everyday economic life is very different. These people bought a house with a reasonable amount of debt and, in return, have seen its value triple (or more) over their lifetimes; getting a university degree was affordable because they didn't need loans and, even without formal qualifications, jobs were plentiful and paid well. Many people recognize that members of the younger generation do not have access to the same kind of life as their parents. Debt was once an option, a choice, something that could be managed with buoyant incomes and that would deliver wealth gains. Today debt is a necessity and, for many people, the prospect of ever being free from debt is very unlikely.

This book is for those readers who are puzzled by this new inequality that debt creates and want to know more. More importantly, this book is for those readers who want to break the chains of debt because indebtedness is causing harm – to them as to the wider economy. It gives pragmatic examples of implementing already widely used methods of debt cancellation that, when applied to households, will forge an alternative path to economic renewal. In sum, this book is for those readers who want con-

crete ideas on how to end debt-dependent growth.
The aim is to start a conversation about transforming monetary governance in ways that ensure that
credit serves a useful purpose in the economy and,
importantly, does not generate harm.

Hacking the Global Financial System

To understand how abolishing household debt will
work, we must first understand how the global
financial system operates. The limits of space make
an in-depth explanation of the contemporary global
monetary system impossible. I will offer instead a
working metaphor to help the reader to understand
how credit operates and what debt does to the
economy and to society. Think of credit as water
and of the monetary system as an irrigation system;
the national political economy is like one large farm
with many different types of crops that is part of a
larger global system full of farms and crops in need
of water. Credit flows like water, which means that
debt acts like a force that changes its surroundings.
Water can allow crops to flourish or it can flood
the land so nothing can grow. In the same way,
credit can allow human activity to flourish, or it
can drown it in debt. How credit flows through

the economy is determined by the irrigation system built by financial institutions and managed by central banks. The irrigation system determines who gets credit and at what price. In other words, it influences where the credit – water – flows and at what rate, through the economy.

Chapter 1 explains how credit 'makes money' when debt contracts are signed. Therefore, when we think of credit as water, it exists in digital form, and the millions of digits on spreadsheets are the drops of water that form the proverbial ocean of debt. Hence credit and debt are not scarce, as water can be, during a drought; rather credit and debt are plentiful in the digital economy of banking. There seems to be almost no limit to the amount of credit that can be created, and most debt exists almost entirely in a digital world of payment systems, electronic ledgers and server farms. When money is created by opening new debt deposit accounts, it flows to various sectors and segments of the population through different channels and is charged at different rates of interest. Sometimes this flow of credit creates fertile ground for economic activity to flourish through investment; at other times it creates areas that are drowning in debt, or feeds asset market speculation, which can be compared with weeds flourishing among the plants. At other times still, a lack of credit flow chokes off economic activity entirely.

Irrigation is the right metaphor because the credit-based monetary system is not a natural process; it is made by humans to serve a purpose. More importantly, because the financial system exists as a digital world created by humans, it can be hacked. Most people understand the term 'hacking' as describing a form of malicious disruption of computers or of the digital economy. I do not use the term in that sense. I follow the former financial broker Bret Scott's articulation of 'the hacker ethos' as a way of engaging the global financial system. The relevant passage is worth quoting at length:

> A 'hack' is an action that combines an act of rebellion with an act of creative re-wiring. The term is the basis of the word 'hackathon', referring to an on-the-fly challenge in which people collaborate to create something new from something old. In this sense, one can hack a door by kicking it down (rebellion) and then using it to build a table (creation). The idealised hacker combines rebellion and creation into a seamless disruptive act, using each to power the other. The Hacker Ethos often entails using things in ways they're not supposed to be used, thereby disrupting them through creativity. (Scott 2013: 8)

Should We Abolish Household Debts?

The idea of abolishing household debts is developed throughout this book as a method of hacking the global financial system (see ibid., 9). Chapter 1 empathetically explores the nuances of how money, credit and debt operate within the contemporary monetary system. It explains how and why household debt levels have grown so rapidly and how this is causing real problems for the economy and for society. In doing so, it attempts to show the reader how to access the power of debt in everyday life.

Chapter 2 rebelliously puts forward a simple set of pragmatic proposals for household debt cancellation. In brief, my proposal is to make available half of the amount of bailouts (cash and guarantees) received by the financial sector over a decade ago, so as to implement a comprehensive package of debt relief for households. I contend that this bailout of households will finally put an end to the protracted economic malaise caused by the 2008 financial crisis and will initiate the much needed rebalancing of the economy, away from debt-dependent growth. Making the case for abolishing household debt seeks out the global financial systems' vulnerabilities and exposes them as a source of harm to the economy and society. By targeting, through various types of cancellation measures, the different sites where debt causes harm in everyday life, we make a new economic future possible.

A PROPOSAL TO ABOLISH HOUSEHOLD DEBT

The plan is to develop a comprehensive package of debt cancellation measures that targets key loci of harmful debt, to provide relief to people and, by extension, to create uplift in economy and society. Taking the United States and the United Kingdom as examples, I sketch how to abolish household debt by rewriting the existing methods of write-down and write-off. It would start by creating a *household debt cancellation fund*, with half of the declared value of cash outlays and the full value of credit guarantees offered to the financial sector ten years ago: approximately £500 billion cash and £2 trillion guarantees in the United Kingdom and $2 trillion cash and $8 trillion in guarantees in the United States. The fund would be administered through a wholly owned subsidiary of the treasury or central bank (a matter of reengineering existing monetary measures). The £2 trillion (United Kingdom) and $8 trillion (United States) in credit guarantees will fund a long-term refinancing operation (LTRO) for consumer and mortgage debt loans that started in 2009. The £500 billion and $2 trillion cash in the household debt cancellation fund will be used to pool together old (pre-2007) and onerous (harm-causing) debts for a negotiated settlement with lenders. This method deliberately targets specific types of debt rather than specific populations of debtors, in order to amplify the positive impact of debt cancellation across the economy and society.

- *Housing debt* The direct connection between debt and property bubbles is clear. Untangling the mess of debts attached to a primary residence requires severing the connection between higher leverage (more debt) and house price increases. Some degree of debt cancellation is needed to ensure that homeownership is a protected savings vehicle, not a speculative investment. Thus a key pillar of the debt economy would be neutralized.

- *Student debt* Loading up young people with debt through government-backed loans is harmful to individuals and to society. Student loans are distorting both higher education and the labour market in very clear ways. We must eliminate the student debt bomb, which is primed to explode in both the United States and the United Kingdom sometime over the next decade, before it causes any more damage to individuals and to the economy.

- *Old debts* Debts that originated in the great debt boom (1997–2007) have already been subject to bailouts for lenders and investors in debt securities. Eliminating the burden carried by borrowers will break the temporal binds of debts incurred decades ago – which are still a burden in the present-day economy because they represent throwing good money after bad.

- *High-cost debts* Debts originating in the period of unconventional monetary policy (2008–2018) will be refinanced so as to give households access to the low interest rates they subsidize. A per cent balance transfer scheme for households would consolidate their capacity to pay off their debts at substantially lower rates over seven years and would thus create an end point for weaning them off debt dependency.

- *Discharged debts* Non-performing loans, including those already written off by lenders, will be cancelled in a one-off negotiated settlement. This will eliminate the most pernicious debts and toxic loans that harm both borrowers and lenders.
- *Fees, charges and penalties* Additional costs added to credit products, costs that were generated between 2008 and 2018, will become the amount of principal (partially) cancelled because they are instruments of rent seeking.

These debts are abolished by hacking the existing methods of write-down (i.e. using an LTRO) and write-off (i.e. discharging non-performing loans) so as to reengineer the time-shifting capacity of debt. Abolishing household debts offers relief now to borrowers and disperses the losses to lenders over the long term. Creating an end point to debt dependency for individuals, lenders and national economies shifts the political economy towards a prosperous future.

The second half of the book (chapters 3–5) details how debt cancellation measures will be implemented in a way that hacks the current global financial system. Chapter 3 provides an overview of the current period of unconventional monetary policy and the existing proposals to democratize it. It goes on to argue that abolishing household debts requires a shift in the dominant moral economy of debt, in which lenders are bailed out at the same time as borrowers are forced to repay. I contend that debt should instead be governed by an 'easy come, easy go' principle, designed to balance the banks' power to create money from nothing with the borrowers' right to discharge harmful or burdensome debts more easily. This moral economy principle will then be used to hack existing monetary policy methods in order to transform debt from a force that causes harm into a force that is useful and provides a public good.

Chapter 4 proposes using LTRO to give households access to the low interest rates and refinancing options already offered to banks and other financial institutions since 2008. This write-down option will provide immediate relief to households by reducing their debt-servicing costs and will allow lenders to spread the losses to anticipated future interest revenue over the longer term. More importantly, an LTRO for households allows access to the publicly subsidised low interest rates already enjoyed by financial institutions and large corporations.

Chapter 5 proposes specific types of debt cancellation; these target specific types of debts that cause the most harm to households, not specific types of households that are struggling with debt. This strategic write-off will end the 'rent seeking' widely used by lenders with impunity to profit from exploiting state-guaranteed credit without benefit to society.

What Is Achieved?

Abolishing household debts reengineers the current credit-based monetary system to create something new: an economy where the risks, rewards, wealth and harms are evenly shared between lenders and borrowers. Cutting the binds of debt means recognizing that credit is a publicly subsidized good. In consequence, we must reconfigure the governance of credit – by the treasury, central banks and financial regulators – as an economic utility that operates for the benefit of the public. Debt will no longer be the purveyor of perpetual financial crisis that leads to the destruction of peoples' economic security and well-being. Debt must serve a useful purpose related to investment in a better future, which is sustainable over the long term.

1

Making Money in the Debt Economy

A Primer

This chapter serves as a primer on key economic concepts that can make us understand how debt operates in today's economy and society. Put simply, debt makes money. This is how the monetary system enables the global economy to function. For most people, money is not complex at all; how much money they have can be determined by looking at the notes/bills in their wallets or at their bank balances. But notes in circulation represent only 2–4 per cent of all money in circulation, even including demand deposits (money you can withdraw from the bank at any time); all of it is dwarfed by the amount of debt deposits within the monetary system. There is quite a large gap between everyday experiences of money and the forms of money that exist within the global monetary system. Bridging this gap requires a deeper understanding of contemporary debt money and of how it operates within the modern monetary system. The limits of space preclude a detailed examination of the many different types of money that emerged out of the technological revolution (Maurer et al. 2017), or a detailed exploration of how historical forms of money have adapted (Dodd 2014). The focus in this chapter is on explaining in simple terms how debt exists as money, so that we may understand how debt cancellation would work in practice.

Money Matters

Money is politics. Most people think that money or currency is made by printing presses turning out bills at a national mint, but this collective image is as obsolete as the printing press itself. At the very least, the production of money involves lasers and holograms on polymer-infused paper. How money is made, and the scale at which it is made, are matters that have profoundly changed, in line with the march of technology. From electronic payments to the entire digital infrastructure of interlocking accounting ledgers, the scale and scope of the global financial system are difficult to grasp, because this system operates on the scale of trillions of dollars, euros, pounds, yen, and so on. I am pulling one thread from this elaborate tapestry to demonstrate how debt and money are made together.

Let's start at the central bank, the institution that is the manager and guardian of the national monetary systems. In its 2014 spring *Quarterly Bulletin*, the Bank of England makes a definitive statement regarding how money is created in the modern economy (see Figure 1.1). This statement is mirrored by the Bundesbank and the European Central Bank (European Central Bank 2015; Bundesbank 2017). It explains that money is made when commercial banks make loans. Banks do not act as intermediaries by taking savings deposits and lending out multiples of these base deposits. Most people find this impossible to believe because every economics textbook printed in the last century explains that banks do not create money, they simply administer and allocate money that already exists. That said, we know that national savings rates (especially for Anglo-American households) are at record lows, while debt (especially mortgage debt) is at an all-time high. If banks were simply intermediaries, this could not happen on such a scale. It happens because banks are not intermediaries; they are institutions that 'make money' by issuing loans.

- The majority of money in the modern economy is created by commercial banks making loans.
- Money creation in practice differs from some popular misconceptions: banks do not act simply as intermediaries, lending out deposits that savers place with them, nor do they 'multiply up' central bank money to create loans and deposits.
- The amount of money created in the economy ultimately depends on the monetary policy of the central bank. In normal times, this is carried out by setting interest rates. The central bank can also affect the amount of money directly through the purchase of assets or 'quantitative easing'.

Figure 1.1 The Bank of England on money creation in the modern economy.

Source: McLeay, Radia, and Thomas 2014.

Therefore, when a bank makes a loan of any amount—500 pounds sterling, 50,000 euros or 50 million US dollars – the agreed amount of the loan becomes newly dominated currency in a newly created debt deposit account. When it comes to households, a lender issues a loan for a mortgage, a home equity loan, a small-business loan, or a line of credit for a car; the amount of that loan becomes national currency or 'money' that generates economic activity when it is spent. For example, money is made when a house is bought and sold, equipment purchased, an extension added, a vacation paid for, a car or a van purchased – or just on the average shopping trip for clothes or food. Issuing debt is a license to 'print' money for banks. Also, when debt creates money, it also generates economic activity from that debt; for example, you receive a £10,000 loan and then go out and spend that money in the economy (for an in-depth explanation, see Pettifor 2017). This is a very important time-shifting characteristic of debt money; 'buy now, pay later' means that economic activity is registered when newly created debt money is spent and then paid back over a longer period that is not measured.

Money matters in the economy, and the whole area of how money is made, by whom, and for what purpose is precisely what makes money political. It is a powerful illusion that money is neutral – a simple medium of exchange, or a store of value. So powerful that it enables money to be used as an instrument of political power. In today's economy, the reality that debt creates money (not simply circulates money that already exists) in a vast digital expanse of interlocking banking ledgers explains why debt has grown to astronomical levels.

Making Money in the Debt Economy

Debt Is Big Business

To understand why debt has become so pervasive requires an explanation of how retail banking operates through an 'originate and distribute' business model. Simply put, banks originate loans for individuals (or issue loans to them) and then distribute ownership claims to the revenue streams (interest payments, fees, and charges) from these loans throughout global financial markets. This business model makes lending to households extremely profitable for banks and those who invest in debt securities (or in ownership claims to revenues from household debt). Banks – acting as loan originators – create money by issuing new debt contracts. Loans are issued without any inter-ference from government or regulatory oversight. This is the 'magic money tree', where money is created at the stroke of a keyboard and made real through the power of double-entry bookkeeping. Loan originators decide the rate of interest that borrowers are charged, again with only 'light-touch' regulatory oversight. If the lender decides that it will offer a loan for 5.5 per cent or 550 per cent, it need only claim that it does so on the basis of the likely risk profile of the borrower. It does not matter that the bank itself borrows at negative real rates, or that it can create this money from nothing. Interest rates charged on loans are not linked to any underlying rate of the cost of borrowing set by lenders or to the base rate set by the central banks. Moreover, lenders have a legally enforceable claim to collect the interest payments on the loan even if the borrower falls ill and cannot make a few repayments. The ability to collect payment is not contingent on good lending practices, exercised for example by conducting affordability checks.

Debt is big business because loan originators create new money by issuing loans and have an unregulated ability to charge interest rates on the loans on the basis of what they claim to be their risk profile. In addition to originating loans, lenders make profits from distributing claims to the antici-pated revenue generated from these loans, which can be traded in many different forms across global financial markets. Typically, loan contracts are for a specified term in the future; it could be five days, five years, or 25 years. A legally enforceable right to collect future interest payments on debt deposit accounts is considered revenue for a lender, and therefore it appears as an asset on the bank's bal-ance sheet. Banks and other loan originators (e.g., department stores or auto-lenders) gather together newly issued loan contracts (legal contracts to collect interest payments on these loans) and move them off their balance sheet, in a process called securitization.

The basic form of securitization allows banks to collateralize their assets in the same way as many other types of businesses do. For example, a T-shirt factory secures a contract for a million units for delivery in three months. The owner goes to a bank with the contract in hand and secures a loan to purchase the inputs to fill the order. In this simple transaction, the large order of T-shirts is a source of collateral, proof of anticipated future earnings that can be used to access additional financing. In a similar way, securitization allows banks (or any loan originator) to bundle together the anticipated interest revenues of outstanding loans, as a source of capital. The anticipated interest payment revenues are transferred to a special purpose vehicle (typically registered in an offshore financial centre) wholly owned by the lender. These special purpose corporate entities have only one source of revenue – interest payments on outstanding loans – and investors can purchase a claim to a portion of the revenue generated from the outstanding loan pool (this is the equivalent of corporate bonds or equity shares).

In conclusion, a great deal is said about how complicated financial products are, but 'plain vanilla' securitization is quite straightforward. It changes the very nature of a loan, from a contract between lender and borrower to a financial vehicle that has multiple and overlapping ownership claims against the loan originated by the bank. These ownership claims are traded across a global network of inter-related markets, which value, price, buy and sell the anticipated revenues on loan contracts. Debt provides a steady stream of present-day income that flows into the global financial system as interest payments on outstanding debts. This mechanism turns household debt into the feedstock of global financial markets. In such circumstances, the ability to originate and distribute loan contracts is a unique commercial power given to lenders, banks and the financial sector – a power that is highly profitable. Therefore debt cancellation is a deeply politically issue.

The Debt Economy

Having outlined how money is made and how this underpins the power of the financial sector, I now turn to how this feeds into the 'finance-led' growth model adopted in the Anglo-American economies. Initially the term 'financialization' described how the corporate governance of large firms came to prioritize profit-making through stock markets over profit-making through product markets (selling goods and services) (Froud et al. 2001). Gradually the term came to encompass a wider set of economic transformations, in which patterns of accumulation could be observed to shift from productive to financial activities (Krippner 2005). This is particularly true of Anglo-American economies, where low interest rates, private debt, domestic demand, asset markets and consumption coalesced to produce a period of stable growth – that is, until the 2008 crisis hit it (Hay 2013; Gamble 2009). For the sake of simplicity, I use the terms 'debt economy' and 'finance-led growth' to mark out the period starting with the credit boom in the late 1990s – roughly, the decade 1997–2007 – and 'debt-driven growth' to refer to the period from 2008 until the present, where debt remains an essential feature of post-crisis austerity.

Let us concentrate on the simple practicalities of debt: a new loan contract not only creates money, it generates economic activity, for example in the form of the recipient's purchasing residential housing or goods at the shopping centre. Over the past

20 years, a recognizable set of conditions emerged: low interest rates fuelled private debt, and sluggish wages produced demand for private debt to fuel consumption. In consequence, debt was the driving force for domestic demand and inflated asset markets, which coalesced to produce a coherent trajectory of macroeconomic growth (Gamble 2009). Debt acted as a panacea, smoothing out income for households and driving up asset prices, which also allowed households to feel wealthier – at least until the 2008 global financial crisis exposed the fragile balancing act that finance-led growth was trying to manage, that is, a rapidly growing private debt stock sustained by stagnating income flows. As it turns out, the large stock of debt (and all subsequent claims to the interest payments made through securitization) remains wholly dependent on present-day incomes for keeping the whole system ticking. For this reason the simplicity of the finance-led growth is also its fundamental fragility; private debt generates demand that would not otherwise be there, driving up property prices and fuelling the consumer economy through more indebtedness, which compensates for persistently stagnant wage incomes.

If we look at the trajectory of debt-driven growth in Figure 1.2 from the United States and Figure 1.3

from the United Kingdom, the descriptive statistics show how debt ramped up over the ten years from 1997 to 2007. Accounting for the levels of household debt and for how they change over time is not easy; there are no detailed statistical measures for them, as there are for wages and employment. Rather there is one measure of the stock of 'outstanding debt claims held by households'; and this provides a partial picture of the total amount, because it measures only what banks report of their loan book, which varies by jurisdiction and can exclude securitized loans that are moved off the bank's balance sheet. Also, the amount of money is significant and difficult to grasp because it is expressed in millions or trillions of currency units (Hwang 2017). Most people struggle to understand the difference in the scale of money when represented at the macroeconomic level. However, even without a comprehensive statistical reporting, the size and the difficulty of grasping what a billion (a thousand million) or a trillion (a million million) dollars of debt equates with, we can see clearly that the stock of debt escalated rapidly over the past two decades.

From the households' point of view, rising debt obligations are like a mountain. Figure 1.2 shows the magnitude of household debt growth in the

Should We Abolish Household Debts?

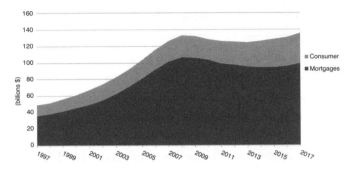

Figure 1.2. Level of US household debt liabilities
(1997–2017), non-adjusted in nominal dollars. Loans
are broken down into mortgages (secured) and
consumers (unsecured).

Source: Flow of Funds (*Z1*).

United States over 20 years. The trend is clear.
A rapid escalation in debt levels occurred in the
first five years of the millennium, being driven by
residential mortgage debt; total household debt
levels doubled from $60 billion to just over $1
trillion. At the peak before the crisis, total consumer debt was $1.3 trillion, then debt growth
plateaued; mortgages dipped, but consumer credit
kept growing over the next ten years, surpassing
the pre-crisis peak in 2017 at $1.35 trillion. It is
clear to the naked eye that the build-up of debt
caused the financial crisis, and afterwards stagnation ensued.

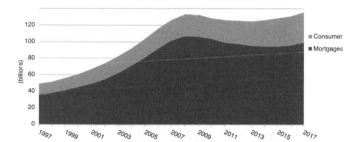

Figure 1.3. Levels of UK household debt (1997–2018). There are two such levels: the outstanding secured lending and the outstanding consumer credit, including the outstanding credit card.

Source: Bank of England 2012.

Figure 1.3 shows the United Kingdom's national household debt stock in millions of pounds, by comparison to Figure 1.2, which is in trillions of US dollars; while the scale of the two economies is different, the magnitude of the debt growth is similar. The steepest increase in debt levels, which was driven by residential mortgages, occurred in the first half of the first decade of the new millennium (2000–6). When the financial crisis hit, debt growth flattened only edging up over the next decade. Including securitized loan pools amplified the debt stock but did not change its clear trajectory. In both the United States and the United Kingdom, the total stock of household debt grew as a proportion of GDP from

29

69 per cent and 62 per cent, respectively, in 2000, to 98 per cent and 93 per cent in 2007 (International Monetary Fund 2018). When the financial crisis struck, household debt reached its peak in relation to GDP, only to slacken slowly over the next seven years to 79 per cent in the United States and 86 per cent in the United Kingdom (ibid.).

The mountain of household debt amassed over the past two decades is clear; however, the assessment of the consequences of rising debt levels is not. Debt is not a problem for everyone. Some segments of the population (the top 5 per cent) have done very well from their highly leveraged investments. For this group, debt is a source of wealth. For a growing number of people, debt facilitates participation in the economy. If the young wish to get a university education or buy their first home, very high debt levels are a necessity. For them, debt is the means to achieve a middle-class lifestyle. For others, debt is how they pay the bills from month to month; it is for consumption. For others still, for example elderly people, singletons, single parents, or low- and middle-income households, debt is a safety net. In the United States, medical debt is a significant burden for many; in the United Kingdom, debt incurred during unemployment is a leading cause of financial distress.

Making Money in the Debt Economy

Importantly, it is not the households with the greatest amount of debt (in absolute terms) that experience the most negative effects of debt. On the contrary: highly leveraged households are often making profits directly from their debt-leveraged investments. It is people with relatively small debts who struggle and are most likely to experience harm from debt – harm that stems from the material and emotional sacrifices required to meet their repayments. Also, small debtors do not generate revenue or create wealth, and this amplifies their existing income and wealth inequalities. Most households have no direct financial investments and therefore use their primary residence as their main source of wealth. Debt linked to wealth generation via the primary residence is the single largest source of legitimacy for finance-driven growth. At the same time, it is the leading cause of the current housing crisis. There are winners and losers in the debt economy.

Debt dependency cannot last

Assessing the outcomes and effects of rising debt levels is not straightforward; a simple cost–benefit analysis will not do. There is no use trying to find the point at which a 'good' amount of credit becomes a 'bad' amount of debt. This amount does not exist because it is a moving target. Rather, debt creates wealth for specific groups and harms others. It is better to think of the debt economy as an overlapping set of dependencies on debt – of financial institutions (as a major profit centre), of households (which must sustain their standard of living), and of governments (which must drive economic growth). What makes households a central pillar of debt-led growth is the monthly remittance of their current income to global financial markets, either as interest payments on debts (mortgages and consumer loans) or as income claims on debt securities (via the ownership claims on securitized pools discussed earlier). From this constellation of forces, debt has emerged as a panacea for governments that seek growth, for financial institutions that seek profit, and for the wealthiest segment of households with significant financial assets. Yet at the same time debt has become a poison pill for an ever-growing number of households, whose financial security it destroys. As household debt levels rise year on year, an ever larger segment of the population is harmed by debt, which has a negative effect on the entire economy.

Debt is not a static stock of claims; debt has a kinetic energy and can easily transgress boundaries between the state (public sphere), the market (private sphere), and society (cultural sphere). Current economic understandings of debt represent it as a stock of outstanding claims against a flow of household income. This static representation obscures the ways in which debt acts as a transformative force. We can observe the effects of debt's presence as it changes and reconfigures the political economic space around it. Debt has agency to effect change; it is not just a static stock of outstanding balances set against a flow of anticipated interest payments. Much like water, debt is a force with the capacity to instigate change in its environment.

The power of finance in daily life is not confined to macroeconomic structures; it is mediated through cultural conversations that make finance the legitimate means by which individuals access and participate in the economy (Langley 2008). Debt has many entanglements in everyday life. It can be a source of wealth, consumption and welfare, but it can also be a source of harm and material loss. When we look closely at the sites where debt is entangled in the daily lives of households, we find mortgages to access housing, student loans to access education, consumer debts to fund spending and to provide a safety net. These sites are the material connection with the profit centres of the global financial system; and rising indebtedness gives us a glimpse of the limits of debt-driven expansion. The power relations of debt are transmitted through a variety of media that create dependencies. The demands of debt are made via legal and moral claims, which trigger distinct emotions like shame and fear, but also via the imposition of conditions of market citizenship, such as having a good credit rating.

When we think about the problems (or the harm) that debt causes, these are both 'big-picture' economic problems and 'small-scale' personal ones, because debt is a social force acting upon people. We can see the impact of the debt economy in the harm inflicted on people by the 2008 financial crisis and by the ensuing period of austerity, which continues into the present day. The debt economy is in a vice grip of countervailing forces. The forces of personally experienced indebtedness are refracted onto the national economy and from there onto the global financial system.

Debt has so many entanglements in everyday life that there is no path out of the financial crisis that will not induce yet another financial crisis, bound to create new forms of harm and insecurity. For example, if every person struggling with debt decided to pay down their debts, the national economy would be plunged into depression, the global economy following closely behind. However, if every person struggling with debt continues to take on more debt to maintain his or her standard of living, soon there will be rising insolvency rates. Currently most households keep up their debt repayments. However, by doing so, they are robbing the economy of its vitality by regularly remitting a growing portion of their present-day income to pay debts that have fuelled past economic activity: these payments are thousands of small pinpricks that bleed the economy, and these are the underlying cause of the entrenched economic malaise in Anglo-America. If, or when, for whatever reason, the same people who are today able to service their debts become unable to make these regular repayments, a worse scenario unfolds. Rising default rates on any one of the many types of loans that households have add to the portfolio of non-performing loans on bank balance sheets.

As the 2008 financial crisis revealed, the elaborate network of financial claims flowing through the global financial system is vulnerable to default on even small-scale retail loans, as exemplified in the United States subprime mortgage loans. Rising default rates on a small portfolio of retail loans would, once again, set off sparks that could light another fire storm that will blaze across global markets. The threat of another financial crisis looms large, but living in fear of another economic catastrophe is not a successful way of governing or organizing the economy and society.

Financial melancholia is not your run-of-the-mill Great Depression

The Great Depression of 1929 was a watershed in modern political economy: the laissez-faire economic model of liberalism was debunked, as it became mired in systemic crisis. It was not until 1933 that stagnation ended – with the New Deal, which ushered in a period of postwar global economic stability and prosperity. Today we are living in the aftermath of the 2008 financial crisis, which has mired us in systematic economic malaise just as much as the Great Depression has. However, the root problem is debt dependency because it facilitates a much broader set of problems, best understood as 'financial melancholia' (Davies, Montgomerie, and Wallin 2015). This concept was initially developed to explain the connection between indebtedness and mental health as reflecting the 'lived experience of indebtedness, in which the psychological syndrome of being trapped by past debt obligations manifests across the macro-economy to entrench malaise' (ibid., 12). Just as the descriptor 'Great Depression' highlighted the fact that the lack of investor confidence 'depressed' economic vitality, the term 'financial melancholia' puts the finger on the exact nature of the cumulative economic effects of the debt economy and the harm they incorporate. Specifically, financial melancholia makes clear how the effects of debt are experienced across the scales of the household and the macroeconomy. Doing so highlights how the household economy projects onto the national economy, not simply through measures of aggregate demand or debt-to-GDP and debt-to-income ratios, but through the sociological and psychological impact that widespread indebtedness creates.

Drawing a connection between the historical conditions of debt-driven growth and the current situation makes it possible to recognize the generalized economic malaise caused by unprecedented levels of household debt. We are gripped by the effects of the household debt, which overhangs the economy and society. Inasmuch as depression can manifest itself in a sense of powerlessness, financial melancholia is not just the symptom of another 'great depression'; it adds a sense of inadequacy, a heightened responsibility for one's own failures (and for those of others), and a general inability to act deliberately towards the future. Rather than mourn the past as a failure of finance-driven growth, we are forced to accept the inevitability of the debt that we incurred in the lead-up to the crisis.

The debt economy has fostered a particular form of economic fatalism: a future that looks exactly like the present – living one month to the next, making payments but without hope for anything better. The psychological dimension of financial or economic crises is well known. Charles Kindleberger's (2000) famous *Manias, Panics and Crashes: A History of Financial Crises* uses specific psychological metaphors to explain market activity as cycles of euphoria followed by depression. This image is echoed in John Maynard Keynes' concept of 'animal spirits', which explains that the human tendency to act is not rational but instinctive. The same imagery of boom and bust cycles is linked to the impulses of people and informs the speculative behaviour that must be controlled if a market is to be stable (Keynes 1936, 160–1). It was John Kenneth Galbraith's description of the Great Depression in *The Great Crash, 1929* (published in 1955) that provided the standard understanding of this crisis. In the same way, Robert Shiller's (2000) *Irrational Exuberance* explains the emotional and anxious tendencies that lead to speculation on ever-rising asset values. The psychological dimension of collective economic activity is a thread that can be pulled from these texts to emphasize the inherent social content of economic activity, if we want to ensure that a crisis is not considered just the exception to the (rational market) rule.

Since the 2008 global financial crisis, the financial industries of the economies of North America and Europe have enjoyed an unprecedented amount of public subsidy, in the hope of shoring up confidence in this strategically important sector. This public subsidy feeds the overlapping dependency on debt-driven growth, the very cause of the financial crisis. Therefore the question of what to do about indebtedness is the central economic problem that must be dealt with. The entire economy, just like growing swathes of the population, is dependent on indebtedness for its capacity to continue to hope preventing another debt-induced crisis and to act accordingly. This is not just logically incoherent, it is causing real harm to people. There is great hypocrisy in expecting households to absorb public spending cuts, job losses and wage stagnation and yet continuing to use debt so as to consume as if the economy were booming. This situation cannot last forever.

Austerity ensures that public policy supports debt-driven growth out of fear of causing another, more severe financial crisis. We accept the harm that debt causes because we believe we are responsible for it, rather than recognizing that borrowers need the same bailout that the lenders received almost a decade ago. Today's economy suffers from acute financial melancholia, which manifests as a cumulative effect of the intertwined temporal and moral dimensions of debt, woven into the fabric of everyday life. These big-picture economic structures meet everyday practices of moral responsibility in a very dysfunctional way, because they feed only a continued dependency on debt. Breaking free from debt dependence requires cutting the many debt entanglements of everyday life. Even the promise of a different future will go a long way in improving the deeply entrenched economic malaise that expresses itself as collective financial melancholia.

2

The Case for and against Abolishing Household Debt

This chapter outlines the cases for and against abolishing household debt. I argue that abolishing household debt is the most direct and effective method of treating financial melancholia, which is the collective manifestation of the negative economic and social effect that the permanently rising levels of indebtedness have on people in their daily lives. A clear proposal for targeting specific types of debts rather than specific populations of debtors is presented as a direct means of ending debt dependencies – the root problem that caused this entrenched economic malaise. The chapter concludes by considering the objections to debt cancellation that are likely to be raised by those who believe that finance-driven growth should remain intact.

Should We Abolish Household Debts?

Cutting the Gordian Knot

The Gordian knot legend comes from the Phrygian tradition and tells the story of poor peasant Gordius who arrived with his wife and oxcart to a public square in Phrygia, thus fulfilling the oracle's decree that the future king would come through the city gates on a wagon. Upon being crowned king, Gordius dedicated his oxcart to Zeus, tying it to the temple with a particularly intricate knot; he did this because the oracle predicted that whoever untied the knot would rule over the whole of Asia. The city was named Gordium and became Phrygia's capital. According to Greek legend and biographers of Alexander the Great, after many unsuccessful attempts to untie the knot, Alexander himself arrived and cut the knot, although it seemed impossible that an impetuous general no older than 23 could solve such a puzzle. As reports go, he confidently walked up to the oxcart, observing that it made no difference *how* the ropes are untied, then drew his sword and severed the knot in one stroke, right through the middle. As a student of Aristotle, Alexander was well versed in logic and could exercise reasoning both in mathematics and in puzzles. He would be familiar with the ancient Greek problem of squaring a circle, for example.

Rather than manipulating the knot by trying to untangle every thread, he cut it in the same way he would square a circle: by not restricting himself to the stipulated tools (ruler and compass in the case of the circle). Therefore the phrase 'cutting the Gordian knot' came to symbolize situations where a puzzle is solved not on its own terrain, as it were, but by thinking creatively, outside the box. Cutting the Gordian knot means coming up with a simple and effective solution to a complex, intricate problem.

Abolishing household debts is a modern-day equivalent of cutting the Gordian knot that the debt economy represents. Cancelling debt is a simple and direct way of ending the problems caused by indebtedness and is easier than untangling the intricate web of ownership claims against household debts that criss-cross the globe as debt securities. Cancelling a large portion of the debts cuts off a key support structure for the web. Opponents of debt cancellation have a host of objections, but chief among them is the threat that cancelling debts will trigger another major financial crisis; therefore – they reason – dealing with debt must involve a slow and intricate plan of untangling it from its negative consequences. We can retort that another financial crisis is inevitable (that is why the threat is so credible), but it will come whether or not household debt cancellation occurs.

The Case for Abolishing Household Debt

The case for abolishing household debt is, first, an economic one; it will unravel the finance-led growth regime that perpetuates the crisis and imposes austerity. Second, debt cancellation will create political change by redesigning the financial system so as to divide the harm generated by the debt crisis evenly between lenders and borrowers; this will hopefully restore banking to its role as an economic institution that serves a purpose in society, removing it from its current position, which is just to enable rent-seeking. This brings me right back to the starting point of chapter 1, which explained how money is created and why debt is big business. Household or private debt is a major profit centre for the global financial system, because it creates a pathway that reaches down to the intimacies of everyday life. Debt cancellation hacks the current power relations of debt. Table 2.1 provides the most simplistic calculation of the public support for the financial services sector during the financial crisis of 2008. This calculation does not represent the total cost

Table 2.1. Basic costs of the bailout

		2008/9	2017/18
United Kingdom		£ (billions)	
	Bailout (cash outlay)	133	46
	Guarantees	1,029	12
	Total	1,162	58
United States		$ (billions)	
	Bailout (cash outlay)	4,600	3,500
	Guarantees	16,900	9,500

Source: For the United Kingdom: the National Audit Office; for the United States: the Office of the Special Inspector General for the Troubled Asset Relief Program.

of the financial sector rescue or of the crisis itself, because that would have to include indirect costs (unemployment and loss of wealth) or ongoing support through monetary policy ten years after the crisis.

My modest proposal is to create a household debt cancellation fund that starts with half of the declared value of cash outlays and the full value of credit guarantees offered to the financial sector ten years ago: approximately £500 billion (GBP) in cash and £2 trillion in guarantees in the United Kingdom; and $2 trillion in cash and $8 trillion in guarantees in the United States. Taking half the amount of bailout required for the financial sector and applying it as bailout for the household sector will, I argue, generate more uplift in the economy than the 2008 bailout in a shorter period; and, crucially, it will begin to unwind the Anglo-American economies' dependence on debt to generate growth. Next, a comprehensive package of household-level debt cancellations that targets key loci of indebtedness must be developed to ensure maximum benefit to households and, by extension, to the economy and to society. In particular, I advocate focusing on cancelling specific types of debt held by households and not targeting households that are categorized as heavily indebted or 'overindebted' (Bryan, Taylor, and Veliziotis 2011; Fondeville, Özdemir, and Ward 2010). This approach seeks to amplify the effect of debt cancellation across the household sector, not to confine it to a small group that is deemed worthy of it. Different methods can be used to target the loci of those debt dependencies that are causing harm to the economy and society. I recommend starting with the 'low-hanging fruit' – that is, those debts that can be easily cancelled or have a track record of cancellation leading to material benefits – because this will give a strong impetus to a larger package of measures that are required in dealing with the most entrenched forms of debt dependency.

Old debts are loans that originated during the credit boom period (1997–2007); and it is this build-up of debt that caused the global financial crisis. Since lenders were generously bailed out ten years ago for offering these loans, debt cancellation extends the bailout to borrowers. Cancelling old debts breaks the temporal binds that continue to make the credit boom years a burden carried by borrowers into the present day. Giving relief to borrowers now finally puts an end to the 2008 financial crisis and to the protracted period of austerity it has caused. By adopting this measure we offer people the possibility of a new future, which is not 'colonized' by payments for the past.

High-cost debts are loans that originated after financial crisis (2008–2018) and that charge high interest rates. In my proposal, they will be refinanced to track with the central bank's base lending rate. Refinancing is a well-used method of debt cancellation; it is called 'hair cut', because a loan that once charged 5 per cent interest will be reduced 1.5 per cent, for example. Lenders must absorb the losses of anticipated future revenue and, by extension, so must those who hold debt securities (or securitized loans moved off the lenders' balance sheets). The justification for this is simple. Since 2009, central banks pursued an unconventional monetary policy whereby heavily publicly subsidized credit was lent to households since the crisis. Refinancing ensures that households have access to cheap credit, which will give them immediate relief from the burden of their debts by reducing monthly interest costs and at the same time displacing the hair-cut losses incurred by borrowers over the long term.

Discharged debts are outstanding household debts that lenders have already sold to debt collectors (in secondary debt markets). When lenders decide that an outstanding loan is not going to be paid (i.e. that it is a non-performing loan (NPL)), they can discharge these debts, giving the lender a tax break equivalent to the value of the loss against an asset. Lenders have made a practice of selling these loans to debt collection agencies, often for 2 per cent to 10 per cent of their face value. Debt collectors buy NPLs and try to make a profit by extracting payment from the borrowers that lenders have long given up on. Debt collection agencies are well known for causing emotional and even economic and physical harm to people; thus cancelling discharged debts will provide tangible respite for the most distressed debtors. This process of debt cancellation has already been piloted by Strike Debt's Rolling Jubilee (Caffentzis 2014) and can be generalized to target all distressed debt for cancellation.

Charges, fees and penalties are additional costs added to loans that started since 2007 through rent-seeking behaviours developed by lenders. Additional charges do not accurately represent the costs of administering publicly subsidized credit but are an opportunity to make additional profit. The United Kingdom's payment protection insurance (PPI) refund scheme is an example of retroactively refunding fees, charges and penalties; here borrowers were missold or did not consent to supplementary insurance policies for their loan accounts. This process can be generalized to all fees, charges and penalties; but, on my proposal, instead of a refund, the equivalent value of the outstanding loan principal (i.e. the initial value of the loan) would be cancelled.

Student debts are government-guaranteed loans tied to accessing education. The large-scale economic problems created by an ever-growing stock of student debts are seen mainly in the labour market, where an expensive barrier to access to well-paying jobs has been created in the form of a university degree. However, wages have been stagnant for decades, which means that a university degree might lead to a better-paying job, but it does not lead to jobs with good pay, benefits, or the likelihood of increases in pay. At the personal level, this manifests itself though the phenomenon of many young people carrying large amounts of debt early on in their working lives, working for decades before the debt can be cleared. Student loans are more onerous because low wages and precarious work are more prevalent among people under 35. Add to that the very large mortgage required to buy a home, and it becomes clear that the generation debt has no viable economic future and that the wider economy is worse off for it. The debt economy is damaging to national economic growth and to quality of life. Cancelling and refinancing the outstanding stock of student debts would eliminate the threat of an impending student debt 'bomb' looming on the horizon and would make a new future possible for the many young people who struggle to pay the debts they incurred for the sake of getting an education.

Housing debts are loans tied to a primary residence; they include first-lien (primary mortgages) and second-lien (home equity) debts that distort the role of housing in the economy. Residential housing is a major profit centre for the global financial system, because it uses debt to create a long-term revenue stream from households by converting their desire for secure shelter and financial security as a tangible guarantee of priority payment. Residential housing is often the only major asset most households have; therefore housing acts as a source of wealth for people with middle and low incomes. The pursuit of finance-led growth has transformed residential housing into a highly leveraged asset; in other words, it takes a great deal more debt to access the (potential) wealth gains from housing. They are 'potential' gains because housing wealth accrues over years and decades, not over hours and days, as in the case of other financial assets traded on global markets. The temporal shift of mortgage debt brings forward the profits that banks can claim from residential housing (present-day interest payments) and pushes into the future the potential gains that homeowners can expect (capital gains from selling a home and downsizing). Debt-driven growth is reliant on ever-rising house prices, but it cannot produce enough income gains for households to pay for ever higher mortgages (Mian and Sufi 2014). This fundamental flaw of finance-led growth will eventually trigger another financial crisis, even without debt cancellation in the residential housing market. Focusing only on debt tied to primary residences will be difficult but is necessary, because it is the only way to cut the Gordian knot that keeps residential housing drowning in debt – a situation that benefits some but excludes a (growing) number of households from having a secure place to live.

Should We Abolish Household Debts?

The Case against Abolishing Household Debt

The case against cancelling household debt is rooted in an entrenched political and economic interest in keeping debt-driven growth intact on the grounds that maintaining the status quo keeps profits flowing. Having studied the rise of household debt in the Anglo-American economies since the early years of the twenty-first century, I have on countless occasions encountered the supporters of financialization who oppose change and I know their arguments by heart. They are not really arguments; they are more like insults directed at anyone who questions the purpose of finance within the economy. I have never experienced from these people any thoughtful engagement with my ideas (for example, that rising household debt is a problem) or well-reasoned opposition to specific proposals (for instance, that bailouts be provided to households). Rather, what I get each time is derision (she knows nothing about economics or banking) and name-calling (she is a fool who believes in unicorns and fairy tales). Before the 2008 crisis, my PhD research argued that rising household debt levels were dangerous not just to the American and British economies, but to the entire global financial system. The supporters of financialization denounced me countless times, explaining that I was naïve and clearly knew nothing about the complex mathematics at play in the global financial system that accurately priced risk and sold it on. I don't relish being correct, rather I want to point out how myopic and speculative finance still dominates the Anglo-American economies. When 2008 struck, the mood of righteous indignation from economists is best captured by the Royal Economic Society's response to Queen Elizabeth's question, 'Why did you not see it coming?' (see Stewart 2009); and the smug indifference of bankers is captured by Citigroup's 'Chuck' Prince's saying 'as long as the music is playing, I am dancing' (as quoted in Dealbook 2007). There was no *mea culpa*, no reckoning or accountability.

As the debt crisis unfolded, there was no capitulation, only demands for bailouts. If these were not granted (and here comes the threat), the whole financial system would come crashing down. It was Chicken Little shouting, over and over again, 'The Sky Is Falling! The Sky Is Falling!' When the 2007 credit crunch became the 2008 financial crisis, then morphed into the 2009 sovereign debt crisis, the Chicken Little argument was on constant repeat: 'The markets are falling!' 'The credit markets are seizing!' 'The global financial system is collapsing!' 'We need bailouts or it will be the end of the world as we know it.' It worked. Every major central bank and major national economy stepped up to bail out the global financial system. It cost trillions upon trillions of dollars, pounds, euros and yuan – and we are all still paying for it. The sky did not fall, but stagnation rolled in and has not left.

My proposal for abolishing household debt would not just end stagnation, it would neutralize a major profit centre for banks, a major wellspring that feeds the global financial system. The Chicken Little argument is repackaged against household debt cancellation, saying: 'It will cause another financial crisis!' 'Banks will never lend again!' And, when that gets a bit tired, they bring in the high priests of economics to tell you that cancelling household debts is terribly unjust because it hurts savers.

It is important to contextualize the opposition to debt cancellation as partly ideological (the belief that free markets are the best way to organize capitalism) but mostly political (finance makes some people very rich and they give a lot of money to political parties). Debt is big business for the financial sector. Household debt is the feedstock of global financial markets, providing regular remittances of income that functions as a major profit source not just for banks but for non-financial lenders, payment systems operators, credit-rating agencies, insurance companies, pension funds and hedge funds. The status quo benefits the financial sector at the expense of all others, which makes these others the biggest losers from the debt cancellation perspective. Proposing a serious reduction in the amount of revenue expected on outstanding debts hits these very powerful financial actors in the only place they care about – their profit margins. In practical terms, it means that the same groups that demanded trillions for a bailout and welcomed billions more in direct monetary financing from the central bank are the very same people who will say that household debt cancellation is impossible and unaffordable.

Opponents of household debt cancellation deem it impossible because it would trigger another financial crisis. This is true: financialization creates more frequent and severe market crises – just look at the record since the 1980s. It started with the 'third-world' debt crisis in the early 1980s and moved on to the US savings and loan crisis in the late 1980s, the ejection of the United Kingdom from the European exchange rate mechanism in the early 1990s, the Japanese banking crisis that persists to the present day, the East Asian crisis in the late 1990s, and then of Argentina and Russia at the beginning of the twenty-first century. After the US-based energy giant Enron went bankrupt, the 2001 dot-com bubble bust, causing US equity markets to collapse. In 2007 the credit crunch became the 2008 financial crisis, mainly in the United States and United Kingdom; but it quickly became the European sovereign debt crisis – quickly, that is, by 2009. Another, more severe financial crisis is certainly on the horizon, regardless of whether household debts are cancelled or not. What will trigger the crisis is a game of hot potato; whichever market is left holding the portfolio of non-performing loans is the one that will take the blame. The reality is that the global financial system is prone to systemic crises. Pursuing debt-driven growth requires ever larger amounts of public subsidy and state intervention to support the banking and financial system after each crisis.

With every financial crisis comes a period of imposed austerity. Austerity is the redistribution of the harm caused by the financial crisis away from those who caused it. The logic of retrenchment – of imposing austerity after debt crisis – is justified by the argument that 'there's no more money' in the United Kingdom (Byrne 2015) or that 'this time is different' (Reinhart and Rogoff 2011). In practice, for the financial sector to continue to benefit from direct monetary financing – what is called quantitative easing (QE) – there must be spending cuts to the household sector. This became a well-rehearsed argument and is applied against debt cancellation: debt cancellation would cost the treasury (or the taxpayer) too much to be justifiable. Of course, the astronomical costs of the bailout and subsequent rounds of QE are never subjected to any comparable level of scrutiny. Have you ever heard a banker, financial analyst, politician, or serving central banker ask: 'Can we afford another bailout?' 'Is the cost of QE to the taxpayer too much?' No; not ever. The reason is simple: profit is political power. There can be no doubt that a coordinated program of debt cancellation will hurt the profitability of the financial sector. But those who hold political power are bankrolled by those who make profits off debt; therefore such a program is a non-starter.

Opponents of household debt cancellation say that the proposal is too risky and too costly. This time the sky is falling because, if household debts are cancelled, banks will never lend to households again! Imagine life without credit; if banks don't lend to households, the whole economy will collapse. Basically, any measure that interferes with the ability of financial institutions to privatize profits and socialize losses – in other words, to keep the profits they make and get the state to bail out the losses they create – will result in a complete collapse of the financial system. Of course, Chicken Little never asks what is the point of having a sky that is always about to fall. This is a well-rehearsed public relations strategy designed to preserve the status quo by issuing a threat dressed up as a statement of fact. Banks can (and I believe would) continue to lend to households after debts are cancelled, because not lending to households would end their existence as a business (there is no 'originate and distribute' without new loans). Perhaps some banks would rather close shop or exit the retail banking than lend to households after having their debts cancelled; and maybe that would be a good thing.

When Chicken Little is tired of shouting, out come the high priests of economics to explain why the heretics who advocate debt cancellation will hurt the virtuous and reward the scoundrels. This argument against debt cancellation claims that savers and pensioners are the biggest losers when debts are cancelled or borrowers default. This is a clever sleight of hand. Banks are not intermediaries (see Chapter 1), which means that they do not require a savings base to lend. Indeed, even at the macroeconomic level, we can see that household savings have fallen almost to zero as debt levels have skyrocketed in both the United States and the United Kingdom. So the 'savers' hurt by debt cancellation are the investors who have bought debt securities, or the pools of loans that originators have moved off their balance sheets and sold on to global markets (via securitization). The multiple and overlapping claims on the underlying income used to pay interest are vast, almost every major financial institution holding household debts as a fixed income asset. Pension funds, insurance companies, hedge funds, arguably the entire shadow banking system holds and regularly trades debt securities in many different forms. As long as households service their debts, claims on these revenues function as an easy profit source. If household debts are written down (a hair cut) or cancelled, these guaranteed profits evaporate.

Opponents of debt cancellation suggest (or rather threaten) that loss of these profits will hurt savers and pensioners. Given the exposure of pension and mutual funds to debt securities, this is plausible, but the reality is that every single market downturn leads to losses in household investments (or in retail investment pools). This is because, unless you are in the top 5 per cent of households, retail investment pools are 'dumb money' where, under the management of a host of intermediaries, people hand over money every month, whether markets are high or low. Smart money is for those who rank in the top 5 per cent: these have people actively trading every day to mitigate losses. In finance, it takes significantly large amounts of money to make even more; small savers have little chance of making money in this game. Historically, small savers had access to inter-est-bearing savings accounts, but unconventional monetary policy requires low interest rates and pushes bond yields down over the long term. This trend contributed significantly to the decimation of retail savings products available to households and pushed them into retail investment portfolios that invest in debt securities.

Unconventional monetary policy has hugely ben-efited the already wealthy. One study by the Bank of England showed that QE-funded asset purchases only benefited the top 5 per cent of households, whereas the rest (95 per cent) were worse off (Bank of England 2012; Green and Lavery 2015). Pension funds heavily invested in debt securities (or investment products derived from outstanding debt securities) will lose out when the underlying debts are cancelled or refinanced. The scale of potential losses from debt cancellation, however, is small in relation to how much pension funds have already lost as a result of unconventional monetary policy. With interest rates deliberately kept negative in real terms, pension funds are hurt because they are heavily dependent on government debt as a savings vehicle; the money (or yields) on these assets will (eventually) materialize as substantial losses to future revenue of pension funds. When this pension time bomb goes off, I can only assume it will just mean more bailouts for the financial sector.

Debt cancellation will hurt a pension industry already in its death throes. The small savers will see their portfolios hit by debt cancellation, just as they have seen their investments hit by the 1997 Asian crisis, the 2001 dot-com bubble, and the 2007 financial crisis. These same small savers are also being hurt by unconventional monetary policy, which drives down the value of bond yields; but this is never questioned openly by the high priests. Rather, they enjoy waxing nostalgic about the loss of economic morality by arguing that debt cancellation would hurt the virtuous saver (who is the pension fund manager in today's economy) and reward the profligate debtor.

Moralizing about debt is the easy economic argument against debt cancellation. In brief, this argument claims that cancelling debt promotes a situation of 'moral hazard' – a concept economists use in describing how individuals engage in risk-taking behaviour knowing that protection against the consequences will be secured by another party. In other words, if the problem is that households have taken on too much debt (the risky behaviour), then cancelling the outstanding debts will only temporarily solve the problem, because households will go on to borrow again, anticipating that debts will be cancelled again in the future. This supposition might very well be true; it was precisely the argument made against bailing out the banks in 2008, and against unconventional monetary policy. However, the moral hazard of these policies was ignored by virtue of the perceived systemic importance of propping up the financial sector. Put simply, banks are still engaging in risky behaviour because they know they are too big to fail; the importance of the financial sector to the entire economy outweighs the costs. I am arguing that the same can be said about the household sector: its importance to the overall functioning of the national and global economy is such that a bailout of their debts is as necessary as a bailout of the debts of the financial sector – and in fact even more necessary, considering that the post-2008 bailout of the financial sectors has not translated into greater investment, stable employment or growth. Debt cancellation is systemically necessary, and this negates the moral hazard it causes.

Case for and against Abolishing Household Debt

A Heretic's Reply

Standing up for those who are harmed by the status quo and combating orthodoxy with new ways of thinking is the heretic's purview. There can be no getting around the reality that advocating for debt cancellation is an act of heresy against the entire debt economy (and those it enriches) and against the high priests of economics (who tell us that debt is a personal problem, not an economic one). This book is not an effort at conversion. Those who amass great wealth as merchants of debt (and their enablers) will not relinquish their considerable power as a result of a well-reasoned argument about the public good. If that were the case, 2008 would have brought substantial change. My book is rather an attempt to engage those who already know that the current scale of debt is causing more economic and social ill than good. I show that debt dependence is creating new forms of inequality; and I explain why debt cancellation cuts this Gordian knot. In the spirit of the heretic, I seek to show that another world is possible. I anticipate that the high priests – the merchants of debt and their armies of public relations specialists – will proclaim my proposal evil, or simply crazy. They claim to know what is best for our collective economic future and for keeping things as they are. However, I contend that, for most people, 'things as they are' no longer describes a bearable situation; and it is time to change.

3

Making Credit a Public Good

This chapter begins with an overview of the current period of unconventional monetary policy and of the existing proposals on how to democratize central bank governance successfully. It goes on to argue that abolishing household debts requires a shift in the dominant moral economy of debt, in which lenders are bailed out at the same time as borrowers are forced to repay. The shift should favour a new principle of 'easy come, easy go', designed to counterbalance the banks' power to create money out of nothing. Abolishing household debts recognizes that it is morally right to discharge harmful or distorting debts more easily. This moral economy principle will then be used to hack existing methods of monetary policy with the intention of transforming debt from a force that causes harm into an economic utility that provides a public good.

Should We Abolish Household Debts?

Living in the Era of Unconventional Monetary Policy

The easiest way to describe the unconventional monetary policy pursued by central banks since 2008 it to use the metaphor of credit as water in an irrigation system. The central bank, supported by the treasury and by national financial regulators, is the architect of the irrigation system of credit: it designs and plans how this system makes credit circulate through the economy using signals, forward guidance, and pumping stations. As overseer of the monetary system, the central bank wants credit to flow through the economy at a steady and even pace, not stoking inflation but also generating growth. Banks, together with other financial institutions, operate the credit system in order to generate profit. They generate profit by controlling the flow of credit (water) with the help of 'terms of credit' (i.e. how much they charge for credit). There is a mismatch of incentives, but this is not just a design flaw of the monetary system; it is rather an expression of the norms and values that govern how the credit irrigation structure operates – who gets credit, how much, and at what price. These choices make credit political, not simply technocratic.

Making Credit a Public Good

At present, central banks, especially in Anglo-America, struggle to use the limited set of policy tools available to them to revive the macroeconomy; keeping interest rates low and administering rounds of QE is equivalent to putting the zombie on life support. The enormous debt stock can be serviced, but no new economic activity can flourish in an economy that's drowning in debt. It is those who operate the credit irrigation system underwritten by the state that benefit most from keeping the economy dependent on debt. The economic record of unconventional monetary policy indicates that only the wealthiest 5 per cent of households benefited from post-2008 asset purchases (Bank of England 2012). There are clear winners and losers from the small group of elites – the rentiers – with the greatest amount of financial and political power.

What makes monetary policy 'unconventional' is how central banks are using key policy instruments; but what is not often debated is how the technocratic processes for managing credit are having profound distributional effects. Publicly subsidized credit flows through the banks to households, giving banks an easy and unrivalled profit source but loading up households with relatively expensive debts that they struggle to maintain because of politically imposed austerity. Let me explain. Central banks in the United States and United Kingdom, but also across Europe and Japan, are using a package of monetary policies since 2008 in order to stave off the worst of the financial crisis; specifically, they keep interest rates extremely low (zero-bound) and use direct monetary financing measures (quantitative easing (QE)). These are measures whereby the treasury transfers newly issued government debts (UK gilts or federal reserve bonds, for example) to the central bank, which administers them through credit and asset markets collectively known as QE. Interest rates remain 'zero bound' – that is, negative – in inflation-adjusted (i.e. real) terms. Strange as this may sound, credit can have a negative interest rate for those institutions able to purchase government debt in the discount window. For example, in October 2017, the rate of inflation (price changes in the real economy) was 2.8 per cent and the base interest rate set by the Bank of England was 0.5 per cent; institutions with a license to access short-term credit via the discount window facility enjoy an almost automatic 2 per cent premium because inflation is that much higher than interest rates.

Central banks have expanded their balance sheets astronomically because of unconventional monetary policy. An in-depth analysis carried out by Credit Suisse made 2007 the benchmark year for tracking the extent to which central banks have expanded since the onset of the global financial crisis: the US Federal Reserve and the Bank of England are clustered at the top, together with the Swiss National Bank, because their balance sheets have expanded well over 500 per cent in the past decade (Adler et al. 2017). Such a vast expansion of a central bank's balance sheets is underwritten by the entire economy, not just by the financial sector. So far, the record of unconventional monetary policy is bleak, considering the billions and billions of dollars, pounds, euros and yen used to finance the endeavour. The key problem with unconventional monetary policy is that it sustains the debt economy rather than rebalancing the economy away from debt dependence. It is a political choice to protect the profitability of banks and other large corporations at the expense of the entire economy. The consequence of this choice is the entrenched economic malaise that grips the United States and the United Kingdom: the macroeconomy is drowning in debt. Unconventional monetary policy established a moral economy of debt in which there are bailouts for some and austerity for the rest.

As Mervyn King, former governor of the Bank of England, testified to parliament, '[t]he price of this financial crisis is being borne by people who absolutely did not cause it' (as quoted in Inman 2011). This captures how unconventional monetary policy protects a small group from the consequences of financial crisis by redistributing the costs onto society at large, using austerity. The costs of the financial crisis are dumped onto citizens, via the household and the elimination or underfunding of social security and other services. There are also clear lines of culpability. The few in receipt of bailouts and ongoing subsidization are the very same people who caused the crisis; yet austerity is for everyone else.

A Moral Economy of Debt

At first blush the concept of a moral economy appears to be alien, especially in relation to debt. Morality is in the realm of religion or private life; the economy is about money and business. However, when we think about the moral codes that govern economic life, the concept of a moral economy becomes clear. 'Don't cheat, don't lie, don't hurt others; work hard and pay your debts, and you will live the economic equivalent of a "good life"' – this is the moral economy of everyday life. When E.P. Thompson (1971) wrote about the 'moral economy of the English crowd', he explained how moral economy related to the maintenance of community norms and values. If we use the example of food riots, the morality of the crowd in everyday life makes the struggle against market forces visible. In this context, moral economy highlights how the powerless justify alternative versions of economic relations or express disdain for the current political economic order on the grounds that it is not fair or unjust (Stanley, Deville, and Montgomerie 2016). The sociologist Andrew Sayer (2000: 80) defined contemporary moral economy as 'the study of the ways in which economic activities, in the broad sense, are influenced by moral–political norms and sentiments, and how, conversely, those norms are compromised by economic forces; so much so in some cases that the norms represent little more than legitimations of entrenched power relations'. I follow this definition because the moral economy of debt, especially since 2008, exposes the entrenched power relations between financial markets, the state, and households.

Basically, engrained debt dependency has created a moral economy of debt in which the profits from credit are privatized within the financial sector, but the losses generated from a debt-induced crisis are 'socialized' by being thrown into the household sector. In other words, lenders keep their profits and everyone else pays for their losses. However, this moral economy is significantly downplayed by the central bank's belief that it is a technocratic agency that guards its own independence from politics. But there is a downside to central bank independence: it can block democratic accountability to society. There are no clear safeguards to ensure that the central bank's choices are not captured by private corporate interests. The economists who work at the central bank believe that, when they use their control over the credit irrigation system, they are making rational and highly technical decisions about how to govern the economy. However, they are making value judgements informed by moral norms. First and foremost, central bankers believe that banks are the best operators of the credit system and are 'too big to fail'. As a result, banks and the wider financial sector received trillions in bailouts, guarantees, and direct monetary financing from the central bank. This is a moral decision, not just an economic one, insofar as it reflects a value judgement – namely which sectors are worthy of saving through bailouts and which are not.

The most extensive treatment of the moral economy of debt is David Graeber's (2011) *Debt: The First 500 Years*, which offers a comprehensive historical account of the anthropology of creditor–debtor relationships and finds that there is no iron law of morality. Rather, debt is a social relationship that is always negotiated. The competing interests of creditors and debtors is the mainstay of politics since Babylonian times. The high priests of orthodoxy want to uphold what they see as the sacred rights of the creditor; however, the heretic makes the case for the political necessity of relief for the debtor. Which side wins, in any situation, comes down to the economic consequences of widespread indebtedness set against the power of creditors. The philosopher Maurizio Lazzarato (2012: 30) explains how contemporary debt produces a specific morality, in which 'the concept of *Schuld* (guilt), a concept central to morality, is derived from the very concrete notion of *Schulden* (debts). The "morality" of debt results in the moralization of the unemployed, the "assisted", the users of public services, as well as of entire populations.' Rooting the moral economy of debt in guilt is based on the precondition of debt, namely the ability to make a promise to pay back the debt in the future; and not honouring this promise is a moral fault. The power of guilt and shame to enforce the claims of debt against income is significant but does not apply universally.

Should We Abolish Household Debts?

Let me explain with the help of a common dictum: 'if you owe $100,000, the bank owns you, if you owe $100 billion, you own the bank'. In other words, the smaller the loan, the more likely it is that it must be repaid; and the moral economy principle that stipulates 'you must repay your debts' pertains to debts owed to the bank by individuals, not to debts that the bank owes other institutions. Consider for a moment that it is not just individuals who owe debts to lenders. Governments and corporations, too, owe debts to individuals – by way of pensions and healthcare services, both of which are cut because of the 2008 financial crisis. Many banks, to which individuals owe a great deal of money, are themselves technically insolvent: there are far more debt claims against them then revenue streams from the debts owed to them. In the aftermath of the 2008 financial crisis, the moral economy of bailouts and unconventional monetary policy prioritized which of the financial promises made in the decades that led up to 2008 would be honoured and which would not. The moral economy of debt is about determining which and whose debt promises are enforced and which and whose are cancelled.

Making Credit a Public Good

Governing credit as an economic utility

What the outcomes of unconventional monetary policy make clear but the moral economy of debt obscures is that the credit irrigation system is currently heavily subsidized by governments. This fact has substantial negative effects on society, because it concentrates public wealth in the hands of a very small elite (or group of elites). Abolishing household debt would change the moral economy so as to reflect that, since 2008, credit is a publicly subsidized good that enables financial 'rent extraction', which in turn causes harm to the economy and to society. And the abolishment of household debt requires a change in governance norms: the credit irrigation system needs to be run like an economic utility, a small-margins business that operates in a way that is useful to society and invests in the economy.

'Rent-seeking' is an emotionally charged term that economists use to signal when the normal search for profit becomes rather similar to stealing or cheating. First introduced by Adam Smith, the concept of rent-seeking signals a form of unearned income, or income not earned through work or investment: 'the landlords, like all other men, love to reap where they never sowed, and demand a rent even for its natural produce' (*Inquiry into the*

Should We Abolish Household Debts?

Nature and Causes of the Wealth of Nations, book 1, chapter 6, in Smith 1791). The concept of economic rent carries into current economic analysis by denoting profits generated without a corresponding cost of production – for example when a government monopoly gives licence to extract mineral rights or just plain old 'favours' that generate huge profits. More to the point, rent-seeking from financial assets is derived from the political power of banks. For example, legislation and regulations give financial institutions guaranteed profits by ceding control over the terms of credit (the rate of interest charged on loans) and the ability to sell them many times over (virtually without incurring tax) – in addition to the right to create money in the first place. Unconventional monetary measures are the equivalent of the state-backed guarantee of profits from lending (in addition to the licence to create money). This is, by any definition, unearned revenue. Using the credit system as water flowing through an irrigation system, the state is assuming all the costs of running the irrigation system and guarantees against any risks that it might break down (again). It also subsidizes the water that flows through the system, to ensure that the institutions that run the different nodes and stations earn substantial profit. As a result, financial institutions can 'reap what they never sowed' by charging for credit that costs them almost nothing to produce.

There are already policy proposals that seek to reverse the rent-seeking enabled by unconventional monetary policy. The economist Steve Keen (2012) advocates a 'Modern Debt Jubilee' that should give direct monetary financing to every individual taxpayer; in this he is adapting examples set by Australia and the United States in the wake of the financial crisis of 2008. Another proposal, led by Positive Money in coalition with other civil society groups, advocates a 'QE for the People' or direct monetary financing for households (Blyth, Lonergan, and Wren-Lewis 2015). Achieving this could be as simple as adjusting the balance sheets of major banks: all it takes is to swap future, anticipated interest payments on debt assets for cash reserves (since the debts are paid off, not cancelled). This, it is argued, would create a stimulus that would end economic stagnation (Turner 2015; Buiter 2014). Just as double-entry bookkeeping enabled vast sums of debt to be created without reference to the underlying economic fundamentals, so too can double-entry bookkeeping be used to destroy the debt stocks that stifle economic renewal since the crisis (Keen 2012, 2017). Supporters of direct monetary financing to households argue that the benefits would be experienced within the macro-economy because this measure directly counteracts the effects of the unprecedented debt overhang that currently stifles the economy. Opponents of direct monetary financing to households believe that the result would be an overexpensive and unworkable mess: a strange hybrid of monetary policy and fiscal policy. Put another way, if QE for the people seeks to reverse the stagnation caused by traditional QE and to address the democratic deficit that results from stagnation, it should do so through fiscal policy – which is typically run by the treasury department – and with the help of explicit economic policies (Michell 2015; Toporowski 2010).

What I take from the Modern Debt Jubilee proposal and from the QE for the People campaign is the idea of a much needed democratic questioning of publicly subsidized credit. Both experiment logically with the existing ways in which the credit system operates and is governed, both being led by the desire of getting a better result. Too often the technocratic central banker clings to antiquated economic models and assumptions rather than boldly considering how and why credit and debt do not conform to their economic theory. The monetary system is run instead as part of what Earle, Moran, and Ward-Perkins (2016), in a book of the same title, call 'econocracy' and define as a system in which 'political goals are defined in terms of their effect on the economy, which is believed to be a distinct system with its own logic that requires experts to manage it' (Earle, Moran, and Ward-Perkins 2016: 7). However, economics is not just a set of tools to be used by expert central bankers; it is a set of ideas about how the economy works as part of society. Thus the existing proposals to extend the financial bailout to households offer an alternative vision of how credit can be governed differently.

In particular, I am interested in cultivating a new vision for the monetary system where credit is governed like an economic public utility, endowed with a social function, and capable of investing in the economy. This sounds simple enough; but it is a radical departure from the way credit is governed, managed, and made to operate in today's political economy.

Easy Come, Easy Go: Transforming the Moral Economy of Debt

Transforming the governance of the monetary system to make it operate as an economic public utility requires a fundamental change in the moral economy of debt. Most reform efforts since 2008 have focused on the institutional design or regulatory structure of financial markets, but have shown little interest in the much needed structural change: the turn away from debt dependence. Changing the moral economy of debt would accomplish a more substantial transformation than any new regulations or agencies to police them. We need only remember that there were plenty of regulations and regulatory bodies that co-signed all the activities that led to the financial crisis in 2008. Changing the norms of monetary governance requires answering some big questions about the role of money, credit, debt and finance in the economy and in society. A new set of priorities for governing the monetary system can be forged by addressing fundamental points about the value of credit: What purpose does credit serve? How does credit generate well-being and distribute harm across society? Who captures the profit from credit? What do we need credit for? Clarifying such matters will produce a set of norms that can reorient the priorities of monetary governance.

My proposal to abolish household debt creatively hacks the flawed moral economy that condones bailouts for a few and austerity for the rest. It stipulates instead that, if credit is publicly subsidized, it needs to operate for the benefit of the wider public, not just as a source of private profit for a small group – that of rentiers or rent-seeking agents. The purpose of credit is, namely, to serve the household and business sectors that subsidize it. Credit generates well-being by facilitating economic activities that benefit society; and it distributes harm evenly between lenders and borrowers. Credit (once again) becomes a small-margins business as a result of generalized low interest rates. Financial profits are shared between the lenders who administer the monetary system and the state that subsidizes it. Credit must be primarily used to fill the need for the kind of patient, long-term financing that can build a vibrant economy.

To create an economic utility model of credit, we must first change the moral economy of debt. By abolishing household debts, we devise and enact a new principle of 'easy come, easy go' as a necessary corrective to the many ways in which debt has transformed our economy and our society. The 'easy come, easy go' principle recognizes the power of lenders to create credit from nothing and to charge the interest rate and fees as they see fit. Their ability to securitize those loans in order to create additional revenue streams is unmatched: no other sector can create money and revenue streams at the stroke of a keyboard. There must be some counterweight to this unrivalled commercial power. If we don't find it, then rentier capitalism will continue to expose us to ever deeper financial crises, and these will necessitate ever bigger bailouts followed by even harsher austerity.

Abolishing household debts will transform the moral economy of debt by ensuring that lenders, banks, and financial institutions carry the burden of the crisis they create. If credit is to be an economic utility, the moral economy of debt must recognize that credit is made at the stroke of a keyboard. If credit is that easy to create, then it can be eliminated equally easily. Banks have a licence to print digital money, which becomes revenue streams in the economy through consumption; but credit contracts, too, are commodities traded many times over on global markets. If too much debt is causing wider economic problems and creating harm in society, then cancelling the existing debts is the only way to end it. The credit irrigation system needs to be redesigned in order to ensure that the 'unconventional' measures taken by the central bank reach households and small businesses; and, by doing so, it would also ensure that publicly subsidized credit is playing a useful role in the economy and betters society.

4

Debt Write-Down

Chapter 4 describes how to hack the terms of credit in order to devise a long-term refinancing operation (LTRO) for households, so that they may access the low interest rates and refinancing options already offered to banks and other financial institutions since 2008. This write-down option will provide immediate relief to households by reducing their debt-servicing costs and will allow lenders to spread the losses from the cancellation of future interest revenue over the longer term. More importantly, an LTRO for households allows access to the publicly subsidized low interest rates already enjoyed by financial institutions and large corporations. Using long-term refinancing in this way steadily weans the financial sector off its dependence on high-cost mortgage and consumer debt as a major profit source. It is effective in that it targets specific types of debt, not specific groups of debtors: it targets debts that generate harm to society, thereby amplifying the positive effect of debt cancellation on the wider economy.

Hacking the Terms of Credit: Long-Term Refinancing for Households

How does an LTRO work as a form of debt cancellation? The process starts with the rate of interest – and this is where we should begin to understand it, too. The rate of interest is the cost of credit (where financial capital is the resource and interest is the rent). Interest rates are set by the central bank and are the tool of monetary policy. Central banks chose to keep the overnight rate of interest artificially low since 2008, to ensure that there is plenty of credit flowing through the economic system. Table 4.1 shows the short-term interest rates – the rates charged to financial institutions to access government paper (i.e. national debt securities) at three-month maturity – and the long-term interest rates – the cost of government bonds that mature in ten years, as traded on financial markets (not the interest rates at which the loans were issued) – for the United States, the United Kingdom, and the

Table 4.1. Short-term and long-term interest rates (1997–2017)

	USA		United Kingdom		EuroArea 19	
	Short-term	Long-term	Short-term	Long-term	short-term	Long-term
1997	5.6	6.4	6.8	7.1	4.4	6.0
1998	5.5	5.3	7.3	5.6	4.0	4.7
1999	5.3	5.6	5.4	5.1	3.0	4.7
2000	6.5	6.0	6.1	5.3	4.4	5.4
2001	3.7	5.0	4.9	4.9	4.3	5.0
2002	1.7	4.6	4.0	4.9	3.3	4.9
2003	1.2	4.0	3.7	4.5	2.3	4.2
2004	1.6	4.3	4.6	4.9	2.1	4.1
2005	3.5	4.3	4.7	4.4	2.2	3.4
2006	5.2	4.8	4.8	4.5	3.1	3.9
2007	5.3	4.6	6.0	5.0	4.3	4.3
2008	3.0	3.7	5.5	4.6	4.6	4.4
2009	0.6	3.3	1.1	3.6	1.2	4.0
2010	0.3	3.2	0.7	3.6	0.8	3.8
2011	0.3	2.8	0.9	3.1	1.4	4.3
2012	0.3	1.8	0.9	1.9	0.6	3.0
2013	0.2	2.4	0.5	2.4	0.2	3.0
2014	0.1	2.5	0.6	2.6	0.2	2.3
2015	0.2	2.1	0.6	1.9	0.0	1.3
2016	0.6	1.8	0.5	1.3	-0.3	0.9
2017	1.2	2.3	0.4	1.2	-0.3	1.2

Source: OECD financial statistics, short-term (https://data.oecd.org/interest/short-term-interest-rates.htm) and long-term (https://data.oecd.org/interest/long-term-interest-rates.htm).

nineteen economies in the euro area. During the period 1997–2007, the ten years before the financial crisis, interest rates were cyclical: they started high, fell, then rebounded. We know now that this ratcheting up of interest rates from 2005 created a larger pool of non-performing loans (NPL) for banks. After 2008, short-term rates plummeted to below zero and stayed there, until the present day. Long-term interest rates also slackened, largely because of quantitative easing (QE), which hurts long-term savers (such as households or their pension funds). Both trends give banks and other financial institutions considerable room to make profit by exploiting the preferential rate of interest offered by the central bank and the market rates they charge on loans, especially the very high rates that retail credit offers households. For example: credit card debts are 18 per cent–20 per cent, auto loans 4.5–6.5 per cent, lines of credit 3–6 per cent, overdraft facilities at major banks 33–50 per cent. Fringe financial products such as payday loans, logbook loans, door-step lending charge interest in the thousands of percentage (1,000 per cent to 5,500 per cent). The difference (or spread) between central bank quoted interest rates charged on credit and retail credit prices demonstrates the profitability of household credit products to banks.

Debt Write-Down

My proposed LTRO for households would hack the terms of credit (interest rate, length of loan, and fees) for outstanding debt that originated after 2008; this would give households access to the equivalent of a 0 per cent balance transfer for up to the value of median income – £25,000 per person in the United Kingdom and $60,000 per person in the United States. The household debt refinancing fund (HDRF) would use the same LTRO facility used by the central bank with the credit guarantees that were given to the financial sector since 2008: £2 trillion and $8 trillion in the United Kingdom and United States respectively. Backed by credit guarantees, the fund would offer households the ability to consolidate loans that originated after 2008 up to the equivalent of an annual median income. At its most basic, the HDRF would provide the equivalent of a year's median income to every borrower, for refinancing. Consolidated loans would be refinanced at 0 per cent for 7 years for consumer debt and at up to 14 years for mortgage-related debts, subject to small administrative fees. These loan pools would be securitized and lenders would be able to access a simple debt swap from their current loan book for revenue claims from the HDRF. This would allow lenders to absorb the interest rate haircut (i.e. reduction in their anticipated future revenue) over the long term.

However, a debt write-down is a haircut to lenders, because it eliminates a portion of the revenue that lenders expect from charging higher rates of interest on retail credit products. The case against an LTRO for households is the same as the case against any attempt to ask financial institutions to take a haircut: the same would happen. Chicken Little starts screaming that the short-term losses will cause a huge financial crisis. This is true; but the source of financial crisis lies elsewhere; such a crisis will happen no matter whether lenders take a haircut on household debt or not. Another argument against LTRO is the old 'banks will never lend again' refrain: refinancing to lower interest rates would give them no incentive to lend to households. But it is very doubtful that banks won't lend again, if their primary source of revenue is a licence to print digital money by issuing loans.

The justification for a household debt write-down is far simpler than any objection to it: since lenders benefit from publicly subsidized low interest credit, an LTRO for households ensures that low-cost credit is passed on to borrowers in receipt of publicly subsidized loans since 2008. Implementing fairness and equality in credit markets should not sound as radical as it does in today's debt economy.

Reengineering the Time Shift of Debt

This proposal reengineers the time-shifting ability of debt – an ability that can end entrenched economic malaise. As discussed in chapter 1, debt manipulates, or shifts, time. In the simplest terms, debt means 'buy now, pay later'. This seems rather innocuous at first glance, but the long-term effects of living in an economy dependent on the 'buy now, pay later' principle as a source of financing are precarious. Currently households and the national economies (especially in Anglo-America) are in the prolonged 'pay later' phase of indebtedness. Let me explain. When banks create a debt, this generates economic activity at that time – the 'buy now' moment. When borrowers repay loans, economic activity is muted, because present-day income flows directly into the banks as rent on those interest-bearing loans for the term of the loan; this is the 'pay later' moment, which can be as long as you like – 12 months, five years, 35 years. The time lag of debt has important psychological effects on borrowers that are projected onto society: debt creates an economic future predicated on always paying for the past (Davies, Montgomerie, and Wallin 2015). Past consumption, past investments, past emergencies and past pleasures created an afterlife in the present via debt obligations. They might be regretted or considered absolutely necessary, but they are not easily thrown off. And just as an individual's agency – that is, capacity to act – is constrained by debt obligation, so too is the collective future that debtors share as citizens of a national economy dedicated to debt-led growth.

Remembering the moral economy of debt, it is important to recognize how the wider economy benefits from the added economic activity financed by household debt. In particular, we should acknowledge that, without it, most consumption would have been foregone, given the limits of income over the past two decades. Since economic activity appears on national statistical registers from the period when the related purchases were made, the time lag of household debt ensures that the benefits to the economy are fleeting. And it's not only that. The cumulative effect of carrying multiple debt obligations is a generalized stagnation. But this is precisely the problem that LTRO seeks to solve. By offering households the ability to consolidate and refinance their outstanding debts with low-cost long-term loans (debt write-down), an LTRO will generalize the benefits of unconventional monetary policy to the wider economy. Households could access to the same form of debt cancellation already enjoyed by the financial sector: wholesale refinancing.

Using an LTRO as a means of abolishing household debt is a way of hacking the temporality of debt – that is, how debt shifts time. Currently households use their income to service the huge stock of outstanding debt, creating a large and persistent drag on economic activity. A debt write-down would offer immediate relief to households by reducing the income-deduced costs of servicing debts. Securitizing the LTRO loan pools would offer lenders the ability to spread their losses over the long-term. Setting a closing date for the securitized pools (seven years for consumer debts and up to 14 years for mortgage-related debts) would create an end point for debt dependency that should allow lenders to unwind their investments in continued household indebtedness.

Offering households access to the equivalent of a 0 per cent balance transfer deal for the equivalent of a year's median income for outstanding debts gives them immediate relief at the same time as it spreads the losses incurred by lenders over a long term. Bail out households now, and banks will pay the costs later. This type of LTRO programme explicitly countermands the long-time horizon of indebtedness by giving borrowers relief in the short term and by pushing into the longer term the losses experienced by lenders as a result of an interest rate haircut. A closing date for the securitized loan pool must be in place to ensure that debt-dependent growth ends (in the medium term), so that debt cancellation is not used to simply reset the same conditions – that is, the conditions for another debt boom.

Targeted Debt Relief

The benefit of using an LTRO method for writing down the costs of servicing debts is that it can target specific types of debt, namely those debts that cause the most serious economic distortions and are a source of harm in society. Up until now the problem of the overindebtedness of households has been monitored by governments and financial regulators in a way that classifies types of debtors according to how well (or how badly) they are managing their portfolio of loans (Bryan, Taylor, and Veliziotis 2011; Fondeville, Özdemir, and Ward 2010). Typically this is done by creating benchmarks, measuring degrees of financial fragility, and classifying them into groups of debtors (see e.g. Financial Conduct Authority 2014). Targeting just problem debtors with specific amounts of debt runs the risk that an LTRO might be treated as an act of charity, not as an economic necessity required to end macroeconomic debt dependence. It is better to target specific types of debt that are causing economic distortions, for example mortgage debts that fuel the housing crisis and, relatedly, intergenerational inequality. Particular debts are sources of harm in society. For example, student loans that saddle young people with high-cost loans even before they enter the workforce do hurt lifetime earnings and wealth building.

Remember the outstanding household debt graphs from chapter 1 (Figures 1.1 and 1.2): in these graphs the national debt stock is represented as composed of mortgage and consumer loans. Table 4.2 represents this stock of debt as a proportion (percentage) of the gross domestic product (GDP). In both the United States and United Kingdom, we can see the ramping up of the debt economy in the early years of the new millennium. Total debt grows as a proportion of GDP, from 69 per cent and 62 in 2000 to 98 per cent and 93 per cent in 2007. When the financial crisis strikes, household debt reaches its peak in relation to GDP, only to slacken

Table 4.2. Household debt, loans and debt securities as a percentage of GDP

	United States	United Kingdom
1997	65.2	57.4
1998	66.6	59.0
1999	68.3	61.4
2000	69.9	62.9
2001	73.6	67.3
2002	78.2	72.5
2003	83.9	77.5
2004	88.0	83.3
2005	91.5	85.8
2006	95.7	89.6
2007	97.9	92.8
2008	95.4	93.9
2009	95.8	96.4
2010	90.7	93.7
2011	86.2	90.9
2012	83.2	89.6
2013	81.5	87.0
2014	80.0	85.3
2015	78.5	85.5
2016	78.8	86.3

Source: International Monetary Fund 2018.

slowly over the next seven years, to 79 per cent in the United States and to 86 per cent in the United Kingdom.

These aggregate (or general) measures of the ratio between debt and economic activity are just basic indicators; they do not translate well as average across all households. This representation does not capture or measure the unequal distribution of the debt burden across societies, which is pronounced in the United States and United Kingdom because of the underlying inequality in these societies. It is well known that inequality of income and wealth changes the degree to which debt (or leverage) can be a wealth generator. Targeting for LTRO the portion of the national debt stock that accumulated since 2008 will reduce the overall household debt : GDP ratio. But, more importantly, it will amplify the benefits of debt reduction across the economy.

The reality of indebtedness, which is not easily grasped from aggregate measures, is that many households have multiple overlapping debts accounts: overdraft, credit cards, line of credit, car loan, and second mortgage on the home (if they own a property). Regulators assume that households switch between products on the basis of the terms of credit: overdrafts (and payday loans) are used for only a few days, credit cards for a few months, lines of credit for specific, large purchases. Switching between credit products is possible, although not as common as regulators assume. However, the problem that many households face is reaching a credit saturation point where they can easily start drowning in debt. For example, a household with many forms of debt, having used up all the available low-cost products, will use higher-cost loans to meet unplanned needs and additional demands on its incomes. Making long-term refinancing available to households allows those with the highest exposure to debt to consolidate them; but those with small debts can also reap the benefits of refinancing. I believe that this approach will amplify the effects of debt cancellation throughout the entire economy, because more people will benefit from LTRO than if we just focused on bringing relief to the most indebted households.

High-Cost Debt

Making available to households the same low-cost credit that has been granted to banks would render the debt stock less of a burden on households and on the economy. Lenders and regulators want to believe that the high cost of credit is for short-term use by households; but this ignores how high-cost credit is used over the long term. For example, a very large proportion of credit card holders carry a balance for over five years, and many people rely regularly on current account overdrafts. Similarly, payday loans are 'rolled over' when a new loan is offered to cover the outstanding balance of the original loan.

Debt Write-Down

The length, or term, of a loan can be manipulated so as to make credit appear more affordable (the borrower pays a smaller monthly amount over a longer period), but at the same time it increases the overall cost, making credit more expensive (because there are more payments). Offering households an option to consolidate and refinance their high-cost consumer loans will rectify the huge distortions caused by growing indebtedness. The time shift of debt means that, for example, a loan for $45,000 issued in 2009 generates economic activity in 2009, when the newly created money is spent in the economy. At the moment there is a long tail of higher interest payments, as households are pressured into paying back the economic activity registered in 2009; and these payments bleed them dry. Refinancing them will lessen the bleeding. A write-down of high-cost consumer debts can break the entanglements of debt dependence by hiving off the most expensive debts – those that are the biggest drag on household income and on the wider economy.

Student Debt

Long-term refinancing can also lessen the harm caused by student debt and reduce the government's and the universities' dependence on debt for funding higher education. Student loans are, just like sub-prime mortgages, a kind of loan given to borrower with 'no income, no job or assets' – what is known as a NINJA loan. Lenders use the lack of credit history, assets, employment and income to justify charging higher interest rates and more fees on student loans. However, the reality is that student loans are a form of government-backed credit, which offers guarantees and (in some cases) the right to use state agencies to collect interest repayments. In New Zealand, for example, the border control agency is enlisted as a debt-collecting agent and exercises this function by stopping and detaining people in student loan arrears. In the United States, across 20 states, you can have your driver's licence taken away for not keeping up with your student loan payments. The power given lenders to enforce student loan repayment is far greater than the power granted in any other type of loan contract, which makes education loans a highly profitable endeavour.

The most obvious distortion created by student loans is that today's young people must take on ever more debt for the same university education for which other age groups were highly subsidized by the state. Student debt levels are currently so high that most people with student loans will be making repayments well into their forties and fifties (Sellgren 2014). Wages have been falling for decades; hence a university degree does not hold the prospect of real income gains, as it once did. What is more, student loans have degraded the value of higher education, which turns an entire generation into peons (Soederberg 2014). We must end the erroneous belief that the situation in place 30 years ago, when publicly subsidized university degrees offered real income gains year-on-year, can be replicated simply by substituting public financing with private debt. Student loans download the debt directly onto young people and make them mortgage their future; then they enter a perilous job market, which shows no prospect of substantial wage gains or increases any time soon. Refinancing a large portion of the outstanding student loan book – and writing off the rest – is a necessary corrective to the distortions that student debts create in the economy and to the harm they inflict on young people's lives. This kind of harm lasts for decades.

Housing Debt

Addressing the tangled mess of the mortgage debt, the residential housing boom, the housing crisis, and the affordability trap for the young is not straightforward. Indeed, it would take a very large book to go through this quagmire in depth. My proposal is to make long-term refinancing available only for primary residences and only for those people for whom the home is their only major asset. Put it simply, an LTRO should be set in place only for those who own one home and live in it full time. Long-term refinancing would deleverage, or reduce the debt stock associated with, residential housing. The purpose would be to transform the primary residence into a source of security, both financial (as a source of long-term savings) and physical (a secure shelter). Restructuring housing debt targets the small-saver households that use their primary residence as a secure place to live and as a long-term vehicle for storing wealth. If housing is to perform a welfare function, then the equity stake in the home needs to be protected as a form of saving. Currently the equity stake in the primary residence is treated by the financial services industry as a weapon, to guarantee secured profit streams. If all your money is tied up in your home and the bank will take all of it if you default, then you are a very compliant customer.

The first target for LTRO is home equity loans (HELs, as they are called in the retail banking industry), because these cause economic distortions by converting speculative house price gains into cash for households that must be paid back at high interest rates over the long term. HELs also cause harm to society by being often used as a safety net, as they replace – again – publicly funded social security with private debt. In my proposal, homeowners would be able to access a specific level (e.g. up to £25,000 or $60,000 in home equity or second- and third-lien loans) for write-down. In practice, this means swapping high-cost loans on their primary residence for 0 percent refinancing no longer tied to the property. The pool of outstanding loans could be paid off over 7- or 14-years and structured in a close-end securitization (with recapitalization at the 7-year interval). The purpose of HELs of the LTRO type will be to break the entanglements of the debt that is tied to residential housing by breaking the connection between speculative (i.e. unreal or unrealized) gains in residential housing and rising debt levels. Doing so would fundamentally transform the debt-led growth model, removing it from the area of speculative housing bubbles.

Restructuring the main (first-lien) mortgages on a primary residence would need to be a targeted intervention, with specific criteria designed to ensure that debt cancellation does not spur another round of runaway speculation in house prices. In conformity with this requirement, a write-down would need to be accompanied by a broader package of regulatory reforms for mortgage products, so as to ensure that residential housing is no longer the cash cow of finance-driven growth. Debt restructuring on primary residence would be based on a formula that takes into account when the property was purchased, the purchase price, the equity holding, the amount of outstanding debt, the interest rate charged, the length of the loan, and house-price trends in the postal code area of the property. From these factors a picture of costs and benefits for the borrower and for the lender would emerge. Then it would become possible to refinance the housing debt, with the attached condition that any windfall gains from selling the refinanced property would be taxed away.

In other words, on this proposal, homeowners have a choice. They can either have their mortgage debt restructured and hence made more affordable – but in that case they will not be able to sell the property and make a huge gain out of it as a result of owing less on the mortgage, because that difference will be taxed away. Or they can keep the mortgage as is, but retain the freedom to sell at any time and keep all the profits to themselves.

Debt Write-Down

In conclusion, an LTRO for households seeks to reengineer the current credit system. Currently debt deposit accounts are created at almost zero cost and lenders make profit from the terms of credit (the rate of interest charged, the length or term of the loan, and the fees charged) and the securitization of its loan book. With central bank interest rates at historic lows, offering households access to long-term refinancing will provide a much needed boost to this sector. More importantly, an LTRO for households allows credit to operate as an economic utility, because the risk of overindebtedness is shared more equally between lenders and borrowers and that kind of credit serves, rather than dominates, the wider economy.

5

Debt Write-Off

This chapter goes further into outlining how to organize the abolition of household debt by targeting specific types of debts that cause the greatest harm, not specific types of households that struggle with debt. To be more precise, the chapter will explain how it is possible to use a household debt cancellation fund to pool together the *old debts* – that is, household loans that originated in the period of credit boom (1997–2007) – and the *onerous debts* – that is, loans that are causing substantial economic distortion or human harm – and write them all off in a one-off settlement. Through a creative reengineering of the key mechanism for the legal discharge of debts, the most pernicious debts can be effectively eliminated at the stroke of a keyboard. Relief for borrowers and, by extension, for households from their toxic loans will diminish the monthly repayments, which are a burden on people's current cash flow. It will be in the spirit of the age-old tradition of a debt jubilee, but one adapted to the conditions of the contemporary financialized economy. It makes economic sense to bail out households from the same toxic loans that appear as non-performing assets on the lender's balance sheet. Making fiscal space for debt write-off for households – the same kind of space the financial sector received ten years ago – will generate macroeconomic uplift by immediately freeing up household cash-flow in the same way a tax cut would: it will put more money in people's pockets. Uplift is generated as current income flows into consumption, savings, or investment rather than into debt repayment.

Hacking the Legal–Regulatory Framework of Debt

Debt is a social relation that exists as a legal contract between a lender and a borrower. With the debt economy comes the practice of using this primary contract to make a series of further legal claims on the interest rate revenue generated from the (originated) loan. To cut the Gordian knot of debt's entanglements, we must look to the long-standing legal history of discharging debts under certain conditions: for lenders, the history of discharging their non-performing loans (NPL) and, for borrowers, the history of discharging debts through bankruptcy proceedings. Hacking these two existing mechanisms for the discharge of debt offers an effective way of abolishing a large portion of household debts. Using existing legal and regulatory frameworks circumvents the need for new laws or regulations (which would take a long time to put in place) and bypasses the need to revolutionize completely the property rights regime (which would take even longer).

By drawing on successful examples of debt cancellation, one can design from existing fiscal, monetary and regulatory structures an administrative framework in order to abolish different types of household debt in the short-term. For example, the Strike Debt's Rolling Jubilee project (Rolling Jubilee 2014) targeted the lenders ability to sell distressed debts (i.e. NPLs in payment arrears, or in default to collection agencies) by crowd-sourcing start-up money in order to buy-up pools of distress debt and cancel it, instead of trying to collect on the outstanding loans (Ross 2014). This hack at the debt infrastructure for NPL piloted a unique method for quickly and effectively cancelling onerous debts – debts already deemed commercially unviable but still causing harm to borrowers (Ross and Taylor 2010). Another way of discharging debt is bankruptcy, a legal process designed to 'restore over-indebted consumers to economically productive positions' (Spooner 2014). Every modern capitalist economy has an existing legal framework for discharging debts, since the right to declare bankruptcy was introduced in order to eliminate the debtors' prisons of the late nineteenth century. Debt cancellation can be administered through these same modernized legal frameworks. Debt cancellation is as simple as providing distressed borrowers the legal means to discharge debts. A contemporary hack of voluntary bankruptcy proceedings and self-nomination of loan accounts (used in the UK payment protection insurance (PPI) refunds) will extend the judicial processes to include a partial discharge; and self-nomination would seek to refund the outstanding debt accounts without credit score penalty. Both measures will write off the pernicious segments of the outstanding debt stock quickly and effectively, which will generate a wider economic uplift.

A coordinated program for household debt relief need only build on existing legal frameworks for discharging NPLs for lenders and bankruptcy for borrowers and combine them with existing institutional mechanisms, in order to focus explicitly on eliminating debt as efficiently as possible. Using existing fiscal policy instruments, the government would set up, through the central bank, an arms-length fund with £500 billion and $2 trillion (half of the financial bailout) of start-up financing. The terms of reference for the fund would be to pool together (1) already discharged debts (the loan book of debt collection agencies); (2) NPLs and loan accounts originating before 2008 on the lenders' balance sheets (existing regulatory forbearance mechanisms are to be used); (3) a large portion of the student loans loan book; and (4) consumer-nominated old and onerous loans (nominated by extending existing bankruptcy framework to include the partial discharge or refund of debts). Every twelve months, loans should be bundled together and discharged through a one-off bailout payment, until the overall fiscal commitment to the fund runs out. The result will be a cancellation of segments of the outstanding stock of household debt – a process that, together with wholesale refinancing, will generate a substantial uplift in the economy by eliminating a source of harm to society at large.

Old and onerous debts are simple to identify. Old debts are loan accounts that started before

2008; every lender has a record of them that includes the total sum of credit issued and the interest rate revenue received. Using the existing regulatory mechanism of forbearance, lenders can identify key segments of their loan pool that qualify for complete or partial discharge. Closing the old accounts would not incur a penalty on personal credit rating. Any remaining balance would roll over into a new loan account, which should originate, say, after 2019 and be subject to long-term refinancing operation (LTRO) financing. Any type of consumer loan book (line of credit, store credit, credit cards) and the student loan book can be identified, segmented and spun off for sale to the household debt cancellation fund. Onerous debts are those that cause either material or psychological harm to the borrower. For example, high-cost fringe financial products in arrears (payday loans, logbook loans, catalogue loans), missold and predatory loan products that target vulnerable segments of society, high-cost store or retail credit products are the most likely loans to inflict material and psychological harm on segments of the population. Cancelling these debts is an easy way of reducing the economic and human harm caused by indebtedness and is more cost-effective than the bank bailouts.

Should We Abolish Household Debts?

Designing and administering a coordinated household debt write-off can be built on existing models of debt cancellation; such models have already been accomplished, in different ways, in various places.

- The Rolling Jubilee in the United States, administered by the Strike Debt Collective, abolished $32 million of household-level debt. General consumer loans, student loans, and medical debts were targeted for purchase in secondary debt collection markets, bought at a discount, and the entire loan book was cancelled.
- In the United Kingdom, payday lender Wonga cancelled £220 million in outstanding loans from 330,000 accounts. All loan accounts 29 days or more in arrears were charged no interest and given four months to pay the outstanding balances. Wonga made this move as a gesture of goodwill to the financial regulator, after years of citizen-led campaigns against payday lenders (Packman 2014). When Wonga became insolvent, rather than sell the loan book on secondary markets to recoup losses, the debt cancellation fund would purchase the distressed loan book and close the accounts. This is a far better deal for both investors and debtors, but eliminates the secondary debt market for high-

cost and short-term loans. Debt cancellation is an important backstop against the harm caused by predatory activities in the 'fringe finance' markets, especially when the lenders business model fails.

- In the United Kingdom, the PPI refund scheme is an example of coordination between regulators and lenders for the purpose of reimbursing loan customers missold insurance products related to loans. A large fund was made available and refunds were administered effectively. The same method could easily refund the value of excessive fees and penalties.

- In Croatia, the Fresh Start program of debt cancellation coordinated between municipalities, utility companies, telecoms companies, banks and other non-bank lenders in order to clear 317,000 outstanding debt accounts. This is an example of forbearance, because there was no government compensation or bailout; debts were identified as causing harm to people by denying them access to basic financial services.

- France's Household Overindebtedness Commission (HoC) was described as a 'well-designed and well-executed government intervention' by an International Monetary Fund (IMF) report that explored household debt restructuring (Laeven and Laryea 2009: 19). The HoC extends bankruptcy proceedings by using judicial procedures to establish a framework in which creditors and debtors agree on a settlement when households are burdened with an excessive debt that they would not be able to repay otherwise.

- Debt or similar charities could play an important role in managing consumer-nominated debt write-off. For example, in the United Kingdom the Citizens Advice Service, the Money Advice Service, and the StepChange charities have an extensive infrastructure of household debt assessment and counselling that makes them operate as not-for-profit institutions.
- In the United States and Canada, the large network of local credit unions could effectively administer a comprehensive national debt cancellation program by using their local knowledge of county-level or municipal bankruptcy courts.

Adapting existing practices of debt cancellation and working with organizations already in contact with retail borrowers and people who struggle with debt is an effective way to administer a debt write-off for households. Self-nomination is an important mechanism for targeting loans that cause harm; borrowers can opt to honour the loan commitments. Coordinating the cancellation through voluntary means will be met with vocal opposition by lenders, because they do not want to set any precedent for write-offs. However, offering a monetary settlement to discharge a portion of the loan book that is either already earmarked for discharge or nominated by customers because those loans are perceived as onerous or detrimental is a reasonable middle ground, especially in light of the fact that lenders gladly accept government bailouts for their liabilities when the latter become too onerous or detrimental.

But a coordinated household debt write-off will provide relief to lenders by eliminating NPLs, toxic loans, and accounts already under threat of arrears or default; for borrowers, the most pernicious debts will be eliminated in one stroke. This is very much needed. Today, a decade on from 2008, Anglo-America and Europe are looking a lot like Japan at the turn of the millennium. It has been three decades since the Japanese financial crisis, the thick smog of toxic loan-induced banking crisis creates a chronic debt dependence that gradually chokes the life out of the economy. The so-called zombie banks with a large portfolio of NPLs become dependent on low interest rates and direct monetary financing from the central bank. Zombie debtors live from hand to mouth, working ever more just for the sake of transferring their present income to lenders, in order to pay for past debts. In the worst cases, debtors experience extreme harm and psychological distress, servicing debts that lenders have long been bailed out for making. Currently we live in a financialized world where digital debts are causing material harm to human beings; often the very same loans have already been discharged by lenders because they have abandoned hope of getting paid. Fiscal bailouts of private firms, markets and sectors cannot be partial – that is, benefit only a small number of the wealthiest households. Fiscal bailouts need to be for both lender and borrower if there is to be adequate risk sharing between the two parties of the credit contract. This is about fairness in the distribution of risks and rewards for the over-lending and over-borrowing activities that cause financial crisis.

The most adversely effected will be the debt collection industry. This is a positive move in the direction of modernizing retail credit practices by eliminating rent-seeking elements of the industry that are causing harm to people. The debt collection industry exists because of a simple political loophole that treats debt differently from any other commodity bought and sold in markets. Imagine this scenario. You go shopping, buy a designer T-shirt on sale, originally $300 or £250, and pay $30 or £25 instead. The next day you return to the shop and demand a full-redemption rate refund of £250, on the grounds that this is the item's original retail price. No business would grant such a refund. Yet this is exactly what debt collection agencies do. Thanks to a political and regulatory exemption, debt collectors can buy discharged debt at a discount, from lenders, and turn around to borrowers and demand the full amount of the loan. These are the same borrowers identified as unable to repay (otherwise the debt would not be discharged). Debt cancellation would end this special exemption for the debt collection industry.

Remembering the Moral Economy of Bailouts

Abolishing household debts is logistically possible but politically improbable. With its sheer political power, the financial services sector will try to block even modest proposals for debt cancellation. No matter how well reasoned the argument in favour of debt write-off as an effective way of eliminating the toxic financial products that continue to pollute the contemporary economy and to cause harm in society will be, it will be opposed by those who make the greatest profit out of the current fiscal, monetary and regulatory regime of finance-led growth. Therefore the biggest obstacle to writing off household debts is political.

Politicians, policymakers and technocrats at the central bank and in international institutions are for the most part hostile to household debt cancellation. The 'moral hazard' of bailouts dictates that individuals whose debts are cancelled will make everyone worse off, because the relief will only be temporary: these individuals will simply borrow again, anticipating that debts will be cancelled in the future. But in 2008 banks took bailouts for lending too much, only to keep overlending to households in order to revive profits since then. This moral hazard of bailouts is ignored because the financial system is considered too important and banks 'too big to fail'. None of the vocal opponents to abolishing household debts will be found denouncing unconventional monetary policy or bank bailouts. Instead of giving relief to both lenders and borrowers, together, we are indoctrinated to believe that bank bailouts are prudent and strategic but the bailout of debtors is abhorrent and crazy.

The long political history of credit–debtor relations is worth reading for those who wish to have
more context (Coggan 2012; Joseph 2014; Mann
2009). For the sake of simplicity, I take from
this long history the simple reality that politics
decides whose debts must be repaid and whose
debts are bailed out or cancelled. Overcoming the
considerable political obstacles to abolishing household debts requires a transformation of the moral
economy that governs the discharge of debt. The
shame of not paying debts is hardwired into the
practices of bankruptcy. For example, after Lehman
Brothers went under, the bailout of the banks
explicitly sought to prevent the bankruptcy of leading financial institutions; they were funded instead
so as to operate as 'functionally insolvent' (they had
more liquid liabilities than assets to pay for them).
The emotional response to further bankruptcies
would have collapsed the entire financial system.
To eliminate bankruptcy as a viable option for
ending the 2008 financial crisis makes sense when
we consider that discharging debts has become
more difficult under finance-led growth. Since the
mid-1980s, financial deregulation eliminated laws
and regulations against usury, or rules on the rate
of interest charged on loans. The argument was
that usury was overly moralistic owing to its roots

in religious traditions; abandoning these antiquated laws would ensure that lending was rational and part of the 'modernization' of financial services (MacDonald and Gastmann 2000). Over the same period, consumer bankruptcy became more difficult or more expensive to obtain for debtors, a change justified by the belief that more stringent entry requirements for bankruptcy proceedings would deter the unworthy from applying. Some types of debt are excluded from bankruptcy; for example, in the United States and Canada student loans cannot be discharged as part of bankruptcy proceedings. As debt becomes easier to create, interest rates are freed from regulation and lenders can simply 'originate and distribute' loans (which makes household debt a key profit centre). The opposite happens to the regulatory ability to discharge debt: it becomes on the whole more difficult for individuals to access it, especially in Anglo-America.

Still, many continue to argue that cancelling debts punishes the prudent and rewards the profligate. This is a gross misrepresentation of how the credit system functions. It is hard to believe that a debt write-off will harm those people who are unaffected by indebtedness either because they pay their debts in full or because they have no debts at all. This could only be true if money were a zero-sum game: one person's credit would be another person's debt, and banks would be the intermediary. However, we know that this is false because debt is money created by banks. Also, no one will be forced to have his or her debts written off; debts can still be paid if one so wishes. What is more troubling is how the moral metaphor of debtor and creditor may resonate emotionally, even without actual money being involved. The idea that cancelling one person's debt will eliminate another person's savings or wealth may sound true even if it is not. My rebuttal is that abolishing household debts, starting with the most pernicious and harmful, creates gains that are generalized and distributed to the entire political economy.

Let me explain by way of an example. Many global cities have serious air pollution problems caused by urbanization. In London, for example, air pollution has reached epidemic proportions; polluted air causes illness, particularly among young children and the elderly. In response, there are calls for policymakers to act so as to improve air quality. One proposal is for a diesel car scrappage scheme that would eliminate the biggest contributing factor to air pollution. Now imagine that this policy were not implemented on the basis of this argument: 'I never bought a diesel car, so why should you get money to scrap yours?' The argument 'I paid my debts, why should yours be cancelled?' is deployed against a household debt cancellation scheme in exactly the same spirit. However, in the case of air pollution one immediately recognizes that, whether you drive a diesel car or not, if you live or work in an urban area your health is bound to be negatively affected by the dangerously high levels of diesel particulates in the air. The same logic applies to debt cancellation. This is not a zero-sum game in which those who have their debts cancelled benefit at the expense of other debtors or savers. We should not ignore the many ways in which all households would benefit from the economic and psychological uplift caused by eliminating the income claims that debt imposes over the long term. Finance-driven growth is prone to entrenched debt-induced economic malaise; cancelling debt is a viable way of ending a debt crisis quickly. Just as everyone who lives and works in London is adversely affected by air pollution, most people are adversely affected by the protracted economic crisis that surrounds them, even if they are not directly involved. The economy is a money ecosystem and credit is the water flowing through it. The current debt crisis will end if a significant amount of household debt is abolished.

Debt Write-Off

The politics of the debt 'jubilee' (which means organized debt cancellation) is that rebalancing economic power relationships between credit and borrower guarantees justice for the many. In the 1990s, the Jubilee Debt Campaign (JDC) emerged as a network of civil society organizations, community groups and individuals understanding themselves to be part of a 'global movement demanding freedom from the slavery of unjust debts and a financial system that puts the people first' (Jubilee Debt Campaign 2013). This campaign created a new language for understanding the effects of sovereign debt: illegitimate, illegal, odious, or unsustainable (CADTM 2015).[1] Throughout the campaign,

[1] *Illegitimate debt*: a debt where the terms and conditions attached to a loan, security or guarantee infringe national or international law (or both), or are grossly unfair, unreasonable, or otherwise objectionable, for example because they violate human rights standards. *Illegal debt*: a debt in respect of which proper legal procedures (including those related to the authority to sign loans or approval of loans, securities or guarantees by the representative branch or branches of government of the borrower state) were not followed, or that involved clear misconduct on the part of the lender (including bribery, coercion and undue influence). *Odious debt*: a debt where the lender knew or ought to have known that the debt in question was incurred in violation of democratic principles (consent, participation, transparency and accountability) and was used against the best interests of the population of the borrower state (including for war or repression). *Unsustainable debt*: a debt that cannot be serviced without seriously impairing the ability or capacity of the government of the borrower state to fulfil its basic human rights obligations, such as those relating to healthcare, education, water, sanitation and adequate housing,

121

opponents insisted that moral hazard ensured that there would be no benefits from debt cancellation; they were wrong. This legal framework informed the highly indebted poor country (HIPC) initiative, which wrote down and cancelled a large amount of sovereign debt, thereby reducing the economic and material harm caused by debt in emerging economies (Lala, Ranganathan, and Libresco 2006).

Transforming the moral economy of debt can be as pragmatic as agreeing to the principle of distributing equally the chances of profit and the risks of losses from debt among creditors and debtors. Or it can be as radical as accepting that 'debts that cannot be paid, won't be paid' and empowering borrowers to repudiate unpayable debts. This is the moral economy advocated by the *Debt Resistors' Operations Manual*, which gives practical advice on how to recognize the harm caused by each type of debt (e.g., medical debt, student debt, housing debt, and credit card debt) and explains to debtors how to combat the shame of debt by acting against it (Strike Debt 2012). The proposals I made here

---

or to invest in public infrastructure and programmes necessary for economic and social development, or without harmful consequences for the population of the borrower state (including a deterioration in the living standards). Such debt is payable but its payment ought to be suspended in order to allow the state to fulfil its human rights commitments.

are more of the pragmatic sort, in that they seek to make a reasonable adjustment to the level of debt held by households. The costs of the financial crisis need to be borne by the financial sector itself, not paid for by a society forced to endure ever harsher austerity. Lenders must incur the costs of the crisis they create. Admittedly this is a radical kind of pragmatism.

Conclusion

This book puts forward a plan to abolish household debts by reengineering unconventional monetary measures so as to redistribute bailouts from the financial to the household sector. Starting with half the value of cash outlays and credit guarantees, the idea is to create a household debt cancellation fund that is at arm's length from government and is administered by the central bank. The fund's remit is to use credit guarantees for a long-term refinancing initiative for the outstanding stock of consumer and mortgage loans (i.e. loans that originated in and after 2009). Cash outlays will be used to pool together old and onerous debts for negotiated settlement with lenders. Thus, according to this plan, abolishing household debts will be achieved through a coordinated package of relief measures that hacks existing practices of write-down and write-off for non-performing loans and harm-inducing debts. Targeting specific types of loans for relief amplifies the positive effects of eliminating the segment of the household debt stock that causes the greatest amount of economic distortion and harm in society. A general macroeconomic uplift will follow.

Redirecting the time shift of debt means granting relief immediately and spreading costs over the long term, with the aim of absorbing losses into the future economic activity initiated by debt relief. Abolishing household debts provides the mechanism for cutting the Gordian knot of debt in a way that gives some time for the financial sector, the government, and the households to wind down their respective debt dependencies. It is imperative that abolishing household debts accompany a political commitment to end the debt economy. Banks will become low-margin economic utilities intended to serve a useful purpose in society and to invest in its long-term success.

Reasonable as the proposal to abolish household debt is, the political backlash against it will be fierce in tone – but not in logic. Making money to bankroll supportive politicians is a privilege that only a few enjoy. Together with the high priests of capitalism, who preach prudence and moral virtue in the economic practices of the borrower, these few will continue to ignore the malfeasance of lenders. In medieval Europe, the wealthiest paid for indulgences from the Catholic Church to have their sins forgiven and forgotten; in similar fashion, today's rich elites go to the treasury for debt forgiveness. We will be told that finance is fine as it is, maybe with a few regulatory tweaks here and there. The only vocal political opposition in Anglo-America comes from the Trump and Brexit political camps, which see a future in which financial markets are unleashed from the shackles of the regulations imposed after 2008. Even more debt is on the horizon. How anyone is going to pay for it is a problem for another day. The long-standing conflict between creditors and debtors is, once again, the fault line of politics. The contemporary politics of debt tells us that public debt is bad and private debt is good, but too much private debt is also bad; except for lenders, then, all debt is good.

My heretic's reply reclaims the everyday economy as the underwriter of the entire debt-laden capitalist system. The daily life of going to work, earning money, spending money, and paying for debts – the kind of life that is currently that of most people – is the terrain on which we must measure economic success. For some time it was easy to dismiss private debt as a private problem.

Conclusion

Indebtedness could appear as the result of a lack of financial management skills or of an unreasonable desire to spend more than one's income. Today private debt is a problem that a growing number of households share – not because they lack financial education, but because the entire economy is as dependent on debt as households are. When the high priests of finance and economy preach that it is those lucky enough to have no debts who will be ultimately hurt by debt cancellation, I wonder how large this group might be. It is hard to imagine that there is any coherent group of individuals (apart from the wealthiest elites, that is) who remained untouched by the burden of debt, either personally or through their close network of family and friends. Indebtedness is everywhere, and is growing fast. Today's 'financialized' debt is not a bond that unites; it is a shared affliction.

What Can Be Done?

The question is, what can be done to abolish household debt? My advice is this: first of all, get to know your debt. Spend some time making a budget and figuring out how debt affects your household cash flow and your spending and investing decisions; ask yourself when your debt will deliver wealth. Next, talk about your debt. Occupy Wall Street in New York started the practice of 'debtor assemblies' and church groups in London started Money Talks events; both actively engaged people at the community level, encouraging them to come together and talk about the effects that debt had on them. These spaces quickly became sites of community-building mutual support that fomented a wider political struggle against the merchants of debt in society. These two examples shows how easy it could be to inform policymakers (if they wanted to know) about the effects of debt on everyday life and on the macroeconomy.

When we talk about individuals' 'addiction' to debt, we must recognize that this is mirrored in the systemic dependence on household debt for driving financial profits and aggregate consumption, because wages have been falling for decades. Even though it may be practical for people who face the stark demands of indebtedness to revert to practical or commonsense strategies of budget management that pay off their debts, this approach is often fraught with barriers to debt freedom, which are due to the wider structural stagnation created by austerity. For example, there is the phenomenon of stagnating wages and income, the increasing precariousness of wage and income work, real-term cuts to government transfer payments and social security, and the reduction of government services to households. From the perspective of households, austerity necessitates that they take on new debts while they are also attempting to pay down their existing debts. Thus individuals must participate in a zombie-like austerity economy, the undead debt devouring the living cash flow. Regardless of the intent or choices of individuals, eliminating personal debt is not solely within their power. This is the argument against the current austerity agenda: it causes a stagnation that ultimately blocks any path to eliminating the national and household debt stocks. Yet doing nothing is also dangerous; we need only remember that the 2008 global financial crisis was triggered by the rising default rates of US subprime mortgages as interest rates were slowly turned up, just as they have been over the past year in the United States and the United Kingdom. In 2008, subprime mortgages were a mere fraction of the total global lending, yet rising default rates on this tiny loan portfolio set off a valuation crisis. Those small acts of non-payment lit a firestorm that is still brewing in the underbelly of the global financial system. Being attuned to the spatial relations of debt makes one aware of how small-scale debt can, through a series of legal claims traded across global markets, destabilize the entire global financial system.

The structural conditions created by debt-dependent growth are the cause of entrenched economic malaise. Debt is at the centre of the contemporary political struggle. To begin a meaningful conversation about coordinated debt relief for households, we need political support, because money is politics. I support the use of debt audits at the national and household level, to make visible when and where debt is causing wealth or harm. In practice, these debt audits are simple acts of accounting and reckoning that intend to inform the nascent political struggles against debt. Auditing involves asking questions about debt at the national and household levels: How much debt is there? To whom is it owed? What is it for? (Montgomerie and Tepe-Belfrage 2018). In the case of national debt audits, these questions are explicitly political, because they deal with the democratic oversight of monetary and fiscal policy. In the case of household debt audits, the questioning of debt is, first and foremost, a pragmatic response to the effects of indebtedness on daily life. Yet debt audits at both levels can be acts of resistance to austerity insofar as they transform debt into a political formation –

Conclusion

a force to be understood, questioned, objected to and acted against. In other words, by breaking the silence around debt and by questioning its effects on a person's and a nation's prosperity, indeed by interrogating debt, we transform it into a political entity; and the result of this transformation is that the power relations of debt-driven austerity are rendered visible and the effects of debt come to be understood as something that can be counteracted.

Bibliography

Adler, Oliver, Zoltan Pozsar, David L. Yermack, and Stefani Kostadinova. 2017. 'The future of monetary policy shaped by the past'. Research Institute. Credit Suisse. https://www.credit-suisse.com/corporate/en/articles/news-and-expertise/the-future-of-monetary-policy-shaped-by-the-past-201701.html.

Bank of England. 2012. 'The distributional effects of asset purchases'. *Bank of England Quarterly Bulletin* 52(3): 254–66. https://www.bankofengland.co.uk/-/media/boe/files/news/2012/july/the-distributional-effects-of-asset-purchases-paper.

Blyth, Mark, Eric Lonergan, and Simon Wren-Lewis. 2015. 'Now the Bank of England needs to deliver QE for the people'. *Guardian*, 21 May 2015. https://www.the-guardian.com/business/economics-blog/2015/may/21/now-the-bank-of-england-needs-to-deliver-qe-for-the-people.

Bibliography

Bryan, Mark, Mark Taylor, and Michail Veliziotis. 2011. 'Over-indebtedness in Great Britain: An analysis using the Wealth and Assets Survey and Household Annual Debtors Survey'. Report to the Department for Business, Innovation and Skills. Institute for Social and Economic Research, University of Essex. https://www.gov.uk/government/uploads/system/uploads/attachment_data/file/31897/11-747-over-indebtedness-in-great-britain-analysis.pdf.

Buiter, Willem. 2014. 'The simple analytics of helicopter money: Why it works – always'. SSRN Scholarly Paper ID 2484853. Rochester, NY: Social Science Research Network. https://papers.ssrn.com/abstract=2484853.

Bundesbank. 2017. 'How money is created'. 25 April 2017. https://www.bundesbank.de/Redaktion/EN/Topics/2017/2017_04_25_how_money_is_created.html.

Byrne, Liam. 2015. '"I'm afraid there is no money": The letter I will regret for ever'. *Guardian*, 9 May 2015. http://www.theguardian.com/commentisfree/2015/may/09/liam-byrne-apology-letter-there-is-no-money-labour-general-election.

CADTM. 2015. 'Definition of illegitimate, illegal, odious and unsustainable debts'. May 2015. http://www.cadtm.org/Definition-of-illegitimate-illegal.

Caffentzis, George. 2014. *The Debt Resistors' Operations Manual*. Oakland, CA: PM Press.

Coggan, Philip. 2012. *Paper Promises: Debt, Money, and the New World Order*. London: Penguin.

Bibliography

Davies, William, Johnna Montgomerie, and Sarah Wallin. 2015. *Financial Melancholia: Mental Health and Indebtedness*. London: Political Economy Research Centre. http://www.perc.org.uk/perc/wp-content/uploads/2015/07/FinancialMelancholiaMentalHealth and Indebtedness-1.pdf.

Dealbook, B. 2007. 'Citi chief on buyouts: "We're still dancing"'. *DealBook*, 10 July 2007. https://dealbook.nytimes.com/2007/07/10/citi-chief-on-buyout-loans-were-still-dancing.

Dodd, Nigel. 2014. *The Social Life of Money*. Princeton, NJ: Princeton University Press.

Earle, Joe, Cahal Moran, and Zach Ward-Perkins. 2016. *The Econocracy: The Perils of Leaving Economics to the Experts*. Manchester: Manchester University Press.

European Central Bank. 2015. 'What is money?' European Central Bank, 24 November. https://www.ecb.europa.eu/explainers/tell-me-more/html/what_is_money.en.html.

Financial Conduct Authority. 2014. 'Consumer Credit and consumers in vulnerable circumstances'. Financial Conduct Authority. http://www.fca.org.uk/static/documents/research-papers/consumer-credit-customers-vulnerable-circumstances.pdf.

Fondeville, Nicole, Erhan Özdemir, and Terry Ward. 2010. 'Over-indebtedness: New evidence from the EU-SILC special module'. European Commission,

Bibliography

Directorate General for Employment, Social Affairs and Equal Opportunities, Research Note 4/2010. http://ec.europa.eu/social/BlobServlet?docId=6708&l angId=en.

Froud, Julie, Sukhdev Johal, Colin Haslam, and Karel Williams. 2001. 'Accumulation under conditions of inequality'. *Review of International Political Economy* 8(1): 66–95.

Gamble, Andrew. 2009. *The Spectre at the Feast: Capitalist Crisis and the Politics of Recession.* Basingstoke: Palgrave Macmillan.

Graeber, David. 2011. *Debt: The First 5,000 Years.* New York: Melville.

Green, Jeremy, and Scott Lavery. 2015. 'The regressive recovery: Distribution, inequality and state power in Britain's Post-crisis political economy'. *New Political Economy* 20(6): 894–923. doi: 10.1080/13563467.2015.1041478.

Hay, Colin. 2013. *The Failure of Anglo-Liberal Capitalism.* London: Palgrave Macmillan.

Hwang, Andrew D. 2017. 'Millions, billions, trillions: How to make sense of numbers in the news'. The Conversation, 17 November 2017. http://theconversation.com/millions-billions-trillions-how-to-make-sense-of-numbers-in-the-news-86509.

Inman, Phillip. 2011. 'Bank of England governor blames spending cuts on bank bailouts'. *Guardian*, 1 March 2011.

Bibliography

International Monetary Fund (IMF). 2018. 'Household debt, loans and debt securities: Percent of GDP'. IMF. http://www.imf.org/external/datamapper/HH_LS@GDD/GBR/USA?year=1997.

Joseph, Miranda. 2014. *Debt to Society: Accounting for Life under Capitalism*. Minneapolis: University of Minnesota Press.

Jubilee Debt Campaign (JDC). 2013. 'Life and debt'. http://jubileedebt.org.uk/wp-content/uploads/2013/10/Life-and-debt_Final-version_10.13.pdf.

Keen, Steve. 2012. 'The Debtwatch Manifesto'. http://keenomics.s3.amazonaws.com/debtdeflation_media/2012/01/TheDebtwatchManifesto.pdf.

Keen, Steve. 2017. *Can We Avoid Another Financial Crisis?* Malden, MA: Polity.

Keynes, John Maynard. 1936. *The General Theory of Employment, Interest and Money*. London: Macmillan.

Kindleberger, Charles, P. 2000. *Manias, Panics, and Crashes: A History of Financial Crises*, vol. 4. Hoboken, NJ: John Wiley & Sons Inc.

Krippner, Greta. 2005. 'Financialization and the American economy'. *Socio-Economic Review* 3(2): 173–208.

Laeven, Luc, and Thomas Laryea. 2009. 'Principles of household debt restructuring'. International Monetary Fund. https://www.imf.org/external/pubs/ft/spn/2009/spn0915.pdf.

Bibliography

Lala, Shonar, Rupa Ranganathan, and Brett Libresco. 2006. *Debt Relief for the Poorest: An Evaluation Update of the HIPC Initiative*. Washington, DC: World Bank Publications.

Langley, Paul. 2008. *The Everyday Life of Global Finance: Saving and Borrowing in Anglo-America*. Oxford: Oxford University Press. Table of contents. http://www.loc.gov/catdir/toc/fy0804/2007049202.html.

Lazzarato, Maurizio. 2012. *The Making of the Indebted Man*. Los Angeles, CA: Semiotext.

MacDonald, Scott B., and Albert L. Gastmann. 2000. *A History of Credit and Power in the Western World*. London: Transaction.

Mann, Bruce H. 2009. *Republic of Debtors: Bankruptcy in the Age of American Independence*. Cambridge, MA: Harvard University Press.

Maurer, Bill, Lana Swartz, Geoffrey C. Bowker, and Paul N. Edwards. 2017. *Paid: Tales of Dongles, Checks, and Other Money Stuff*. Cambridge, MA: MIT Press.

McLeay, Michael, Amar Radia, and Ryland Thomas. 2014. 'Money in the modern economy: An introduction'. *Bank of England Quarterly Bulletin* 54(1): 4–13.

Mian, Atif, and Amir Sufi. 2014. *House of Debt: How They (and You) Caused the Great Recession, and How We Can Prevent It from Happening Again*. Chicago, IL: University of Chicago Press.

Bibliography

Michell, Jo. 2015. 'Corbyn and the peoples' Bank of England'. Blog, 5 August. https://medium.com/@jomichell/corbyn-and-the-peoples-bank-of-england-755207f8de84.

Montgomerie, Johnna, and Daniela Tepe-Belfrage. 2018. 'Spaces of debt resistance and the contemporary politics of financialised capitalism'. Geoforum, May. https://doi.org/10.1016/j.geoforum.2018.05.012.

Packman, Carl. 2014. *Payday Lending: Global Growth of the High-Cost Credit Market*. New York: Palgrave Pivot.

Pettifor, Ann. 2017. *The Production of Money: How to Break the Power of the Banks*. London: Verso.

Rolling Jubilee. 2014. 'Transparency: Debt Buys'. http://rollingjubilee.org/transparency/#debtbuys (accessed 04/10/2018).

Ross, Andrew. 2014. *Creditocracy: And the Case for Debt Refusal*. New York: O/R Books.

Ross, Andrew, and Astra Taylor. 2010. 'Rolling Jubilee is a spark – not the solution'. *Nation*, 27 November 2010. http://www.thenation.com/article/171478/rolling-jubilee-spark-not-solution#.

Sayer, Andrew. 2000. 'Moral economy and political economy'. *Studies in Political Economy* 61(1): 79–103.

Scott, Brett. 2013. *The Heretic's Guide to Global Finance: Hacking the Future of Money*. London: Pluto Press.

Bibliography

Sellgren, Katherine. 2014. 'Students could be paying loans into their 50s: Report'. BBC News, 10 April 2014. http://www.bbc.co.uk/news/education-26954901.

Shiller, Robert J. 2000. *Irrational Exuberance*. Princeton, NJ: Princeton University Press.

Smith, Adam. 1791. *An Inquiry into the Nature and Causes of the Wealth of Nations*. Basel: Printed for J. J. Tourneisen and J. L. Legrand.

Soederberg, Susanne. 2014. 'Student loans, debtfare and the commodification of debt: The politics of securitization and the displacement of risk'. *Critical Sociology* 40(5): 689–709. doi: 10.1177/0896920513513964.

Spooner, Joseph. 2014. 'Why people should have a right not to pay their debts'. Blog, LSE. http://blogs.lse.ac.uk/politicsandpolicy/why-people-should-have-a-right-not-to-pay-their-debts.

Stanley, Liam, Joe Deville, and Johnna Montgomerie. 2016. 'Digital debt management: The everyday life of austerity'. *New Formations* 87: 64–82. doi: 10.3898/NEWF.87.4.2016.

Strike Debt. 2012. *The Debt Resistors' Operations Manual*. http://strikedebt.org/The-Debt-Resistors-Operations-Manual.pdf.

Thompson, Edward P. 1971. 'The moral economy of the English crowd in the eighteenth century'. *Past & Present* 50: 76–136.

Toporowski, Jan. 2010. *Why the World Economy Needs a Financial Crash and Other Critical Essays on Finance and Financial Economics*. London: Anthem.

Turner, Adair. 2015. 'The case for monetary finance: An essentially political issue'. Paper presented at the 16th Jacques Polak Annual Research Conference hosted by the International Monetary Fund, Washington, DC, November 5–6, 2015. https://www.imf.org/external/np/res/seminars/2015/arc/pdf/Turner_pres.pdf.

Weale, Martin, and Bank of England. 2016. 'Unconventional monetary policy'. Speech delivered at the University of Nottingham, 8 March. http://www.bankofengland.co.uk/publications/Pages/speeches/2016/888.aspx.